THE CUSTOM BICYCLE

BUYING, SETTING UP, AND RIDING
THE QUALITY BICYCLE

by
Michael J. Kolin
and
Denise M. de la Rosa

 **Rodale Press**
Emmaus, Pa.

Book Design by T. A. Lepley

*Printed in the United States of America on recycled paper,
containing a high percentage of de-inked fiber.*

4 6 8 10 9 7 5 3   hardcover
8 10 9 7   paperback

Library of Congress Cataloging in Publication Data

Kolin, Michael J
  The custom bicycle.

  Bibliography: p.
  Includes index.
   1. Bicycles and tricycles—Design and construction.
2. Cycling.   I. De la Rosa, Denise M., joint author.
II. Title.
TL410.K64   629.22′72   79-1451
ISBN 0-87857-254-6 hardcover
ISBN 0-87857-255-4 paperback

Contents

This book is dedicated to Mike Walden.

Acknowledgments

Special thanks to Bill Betton, Eddie Borysewicz, Frank Brilando, Anthony Cappella, M. A. Chiarella, Andrea Cinelli, Cino Cinelli, Frank Clements, E. C. Cooper, Henri de Laissardiere, Raymond Fletcher, John Foster, Mike Fraysse, Vic Fraysse, Dennis Freezer, Georgetown Cycle, Italo Guerciotti, Paulo Guerciotti, Eddie Haslehurst, Bob Jackson, Raoul Jeand'Heur, Barry Koenig, Derek Land, Bill Lee, Gerald O'Donovan, R. P. O'Donovan, Lee Parker, Jean-Michel Piet, Mel Pinto, Sante Pogliaghi, Harry Quinn, Tom Rymanowicz, Rick Schwinn, Charles Shannon, Stuyvesant Bicycle Distributors, Jack Taylor, Ken Taylor, Norman Taylor, Peg Taylor, Leonard Trotman, Ultima, Inc., Stephen Woodrup, Stephen Morris Woodrup, Grant Young, Monty Young, and all those who freely gave their time and expertise to insure the comprehensiveness and accuracy of this venture.

Introduction

Why another book on cycling? Since the bicycle boom in 1973, dozens of books about bicycling have appeared, but few of the books answered the questions many people were asking. The C.O.N.I. book, *Cycling* (Rome: F.I.A.C., 1972), came as close as any, yet it leaves more questions about bicycles unanswered than it has been able to answer. More and more riders are now interested in top-quality equipment but as the price of the equipment increases, the available information decreases.

After owning and operating our own bicycle shop, we discovered that few people are knowledgeable about the design and intent of quality bicycles. For instance, the vast majority of cyclists we met were riding bicycles that were far too big for their physiques. Frequently, equipment had been misused or broken because the owner did not know how to use it. Worse, many so-called "bicycle people" didn't really know their products. Many were attracted to cycling because it became "the thing to do." Because of the demand for sports bicycles, 10-speed bicycles were sold by mail order, in ski shops, gas stations, and major department stores. Many inexperienced store owners selected their stock of bicycles by appearance or because the markup was good. How many really knew the difference between a bicycle made out of tubing and a bicycle made out of pipe?

As we began outlining the content of this book, we realized that our objectives were complex and they appeared, at first glance, to be the subjects of two separate books. We believe that a review of our objectives will clarify the organization. *Our first objective is to "demystify" the quality bicycle frame. We want to present an accurate description of the "why's" behind the design and manufacture of the modern bicycle.* We feel that the whole area of frame design requires explanation since a frame, or component, isn't "the best" by definition alone.

We wanted to supply an answer to the all-inclusive question: "What makes a given frame, or component, appropriate for a specific use?" To supply the answers, we went to some of the most famous frame builders in the world. What better way to learn about the little-known art of frame building than to personally visit the masters?

To put their ideas, methods, and opinions into proper perspective, we devote a chapter to each builder or company. In this way we eliminated any personal bias and, at the same time, provide the reader with a basis for comparison among builders. Furthermore, we were able to present pertinent biographical information on the builder. We feel that the reader's interests are best served when he or she can evaluate each builder's experience and training as well as his design philosophies. This method of presenting the material should allow logical comparison between individual builders and their techniques.

Our second objective is to provide the reader with a guide to the proper setup and use of a quality lightweight bicycle. It is obvious that not everyone needs a custom frame. *Everyone*, however, can benefit from the advice of an experienced coach. Unfortunately, many riders in this country do not have anyone to provide basic cycling tips. To answer this need, we prepared the "how-to" sections of the book.

The recommendations in the chapters devoted to bicycle setup and riding techniques are supported by many of the world's cycling experts. The accumulation of the materials in the book began in 1961 when the author (Mike Kolin) began racing under the coaching of Mike Walden in Detroit, Michigan. For those of you who are not familiar with Mike Walden's coaching success, here is a partial list of riders who have followed his training plans:

Bob Travani	1948 Olympic Team
Tom O'Rourke	1952 Olympic Team, 1959 Pan American Team
Karl Wettberg	1956 Pan American Team
Bill Freund	1960 Olympic Team
Roger Young	1972, 1976 Olympic Team
Sheila Young	1973, 1976 World Champion
Sue Novara	1975 World Champion

After winning four state championship titles and serving as a coach for the Wolverine–Schwinn Sports Club, Michigan, Mike Kolin compared his personal theories with every available expert before attempting to publish the findings.

Accomplishment of these two objectives (individual biographical sketches describing technique and design philosophies, and bicycle setup) can best be obtained when the information is presented side by side since the relationship between proper frame design and the position of the rider is interrelated. For instance, most frame builders design their frames for specific weight distribution. How can the rider expect to optimize the benefits of a top-quality frame unless he or she is positioned properly on the frame? *Although most riders would realize very little performance increase with a custom frame, understanding frame design theory can help the rider to choose a factory-built frame.*

One final word on the layout of the book. The builders included in the book were selected by a number of subjective criteria: popularity and/or reputation of the frame, the importance of the builder in cycling history, unique innovations by the builder, and willingness of the builder to provide us with his time. The chapters are presented by country with builders in alphabetical order. There are some obvious exclusions. Omission of a builder should not be construed as a negative reaction to the builder or his product. We were unable to visit everyone. We decided to omit some of the famous builders who were surrounded by rumors that were difficult, if not impossible, to prove or disprove. For instance, many industry people claim that one very famous builder hasn't built a frame in years for the general public. Instead, a small firm builds the frames and ships them to the "builder" without decals. He has someone install his own decals and the public believes they are buying a frame built by one of the recognized "masters." We chose to eliminate that particular builder from the book since we were unable to adequately substantiate or refute the widespread rumor. We were able to determine, however, that few individual builders produce more than 300 to 400 frames per year. (This can vary when the "master" utilizes assistant builders or apprentices.) The previously mentioned builder had been producing a similar number until recent years when he met demand for his product by an overnight production increase that numbered in the thousands!

We hope that our efforts to objectively present the facts will help you to enjoy reading this book as much as we have enjoyed dealing with the many interesting personalities who made it possible.

Michael J. Kolin   *Denise M. de la Rosa*

PART I

Understanding the Bicycle Frame

CHAPTER 1

The Bicycle Frame

The heart of the modern bicycle is the frame. Unlike most other products, however, the bicycle cannot be distinguished by its components alone. For instance, the vast majority of high-quality racing bicycles are sold with Campagnolo parts (cranks, pedals, brakes, *derailleurs*, hubs), whether the frame has been built in England, France, Belgium, the United States, or Italy. One of the major subjects of this book is the bicycle frame. Let's take a look at the parts that go into a frame, and consider the advantages and disadvantages of each of these parts.

Main Triangle

There are two basic methods for building the *main triangle* of a frame: with, or without, *lugs*. Generally, lugless frames are found on inexpensive bicycles since it is the least complicated of the two methods of construction. Extremely inexpensive lugless frames are usually made of pipe (unlike a tube which is seamless, a pipe has a seam and is considerably less expensive) and welded together. This method of manufacture is wholly satisfactory when light weight is not important—strength of the joint is accomplished by heavy, thick-gauge pipe, or as some refer to it, welded tubing. This type of design is intended for utility use rather than performance. In some rare instances, high-quality superlight bicycles are constructed without lugs. These are generally special-purpose bicycles that receive very special assembly and treatment. The vast majority of quality lightweight bicycles are built with lugs.

The purpose of the lug is simple. It provides a greatly increased brazing area and the benefit of additional strength without a large weight penalty. The lugs in figure 1–2 are a

1

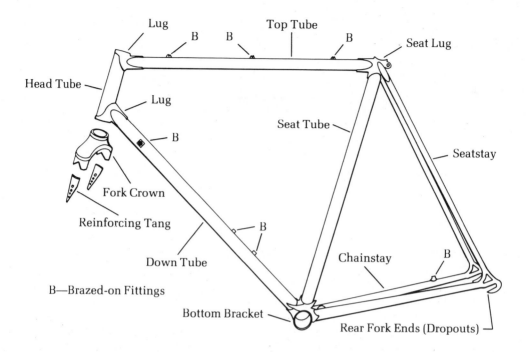

Figure 1-1: The main triangle.

sample of the lugs available from the Italian firm, Cinelli Cino & C. There are other manufacturers who also produce a wide variety of styles and designs including *Prugnat, Agrati, Roto, Bocama,*

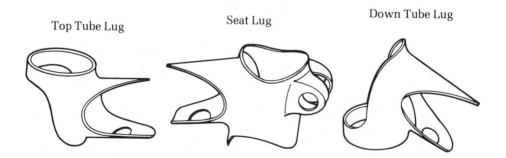

Figure 1-2: Lugs manufactured by the Italian firm, Cinelli Cino & C.

Nervex, and *Haden.* All of the frame parts illustrated in this chapter are from Cinelli Cino & C.

There are two basic methods of steel lug manufacture—pressing and casting. The *cast lug* is rarely used anymore because it is far more expensive than a pressed lug, and it is virtually impossible to adjust the angle of the lug as required in custom building. Furthermore, it tends to have small perforations caused by the casting process that are difficult to file out, and has inconsistent thickness that increases the possibility of overheating the tube. The cast lug, however, is considered to be the strongest lug available.

The *pressed lug* is basically a steel pressing which has been formed, welded at the joint, and machined to perfect roundness. The quality of pressed lugs has increased to the point where they are almost always used because of their adequate strength, reasonable cost, and ease of use. The major lug manufacturers supply them presized for the most popular joint angles. An additional advantage with the pressed lug is its ability to be bent slightly if the builder requires a unique angle because of design specifications. We found that many of the larger frame builders carried an inventory of the popular lugs in several "normal" angles. Some of the smaller builders relied on reshaping their lugs if the frame they were building could not accept the standard 73-degree angles.

The *bottom bracket* also is available in cast or pressed steel. Many builders believe that the *cast bottom bracket* is required in a

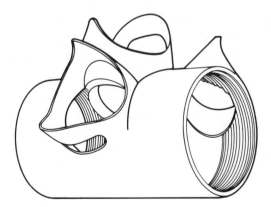

Figure 1-3: Bottom bracket shell in cast steel.

3

racing bicycle because of the enormous stresses that occur when pedaling. The cast bottom bracket (figure 1–3) is considerably more expensive and it takes much more work to produce an aesthetically pleasing finished product. An additional complication for the builder is the customer's request for various *threads* (*English, French, Swiss, Italian*) and widths.

Although the tubing can be joined in the lugs using CO_2 welding of oxygen-acetylene, *bronze brazing* is recommended by the tubing manufacturers and is practiced by most quality builders. Most builders we spoke to used the terms bronze and brass *brazing* interchangeably. Bronze is relatively easy to use, it's readily available, and it flows at a fairly low temperature with a wide dispersion of heat. Excessive heat during the building process is the number one enemy of the lightweight tube—excess heat makes the tube brittle and prone to early failure. A popular alternative to bronze is a mixture of *silver solder,* which is used primarily with light-gauge tubing because of high cost and increased need of assembly accuracy. The subject of tubing will be covered in detail in chapter 2 with a review of the two primary sources of quality bicycle tubes: *Reynolds* and *Columbus*. At this point it is important to understand *how* the frame is built using a set of frame tubes.

A bicycle frame that has been properly brazed is worth much, much more than the component cost of its tubes and lugs because poor building techniques alone will totally eliminate the benefits of using top-quality materials. Unfortunately, if the builder carefully files away his mistakes and does a first-class paint job, it is difficult to tell if the frame has been properly constructed. Before we discuss how to test a finished frame, let's look at the "right way" to build a bicycle.

Assuming top-quality materials are used, the strength of a joint is dependent upon the fit of the components and the proficiency of the person who brazes them together. If the gap between the tube and the lug is too large, too much braze will be required. If the gap is too small, too little braze will be able to enter and insure the strength of the joint. The quality of the lug and the builder's preparation to insure proper tolerances will have a significant effect on the strength of the joint. The importance of the fit can be best demonstrated when silver braze is used. The properties of silver require that the gap between tubes and lug not exceed .003 inch to insure a strong joint!

One prime difference between most production frames and a

Figure 1-4: Proteus Design uses a lathe to precisely miter tubes before brazing. The tube is placed on the movable table which is set to the appropriate angle of the cut. It is then fed toward the rotating chuck which cuts a perfect miter.

custom frame is the practice of *mitering* all the tubes. Simply stated, a mitered tube is shaped to fit around the tube it butts against. The unmitered tube leaves room for movement inside the lug under extreme stress. The tube that has been mitered cannot move. Careful mitering can be time consuming, but its importance is recognized by all expert frame builders. Surprisingly, some so-called quality builders do a mediocre job of mitering tubes and many of the smaller builders (even some of the famous European builders) still miter a tube by hand. Greater accuracy is insured if the mitering process is done on a precision machine. Figure 1–4 is a photograph of the lathe that Proteus Design in College Park, Maryland, uses to miter tubes. The tube is attached to a moving platform on the lathe and set at the angle of the frame to be produced. It is then guided toward the rotating chuck which cuts a perfect miter. Premitered tubes can be seen on the shelves above the lathe.

After the tubes and lugs have been properly sized and prepared, the pieces are ready to be brazed, which introduces another critical step. How does the builder hold all the pieces and at the same time braze them in perfect alignment? Some builders use a *jig* to guarantee that everything fits properly, doesn't move around when being brazed, and maintains perfect alignment during the brazing process. A typical jig is relatively simple and usually is designed and constructed by each individual frame

Figure 1-5: Fork jigs are usually fairly simple and variations between builders are slight. This is a jig used by Bob Jackson (chapter 5). The fork has just been brazed and therefore has a very rough appearance.

builder. The variation in jigs reflects different construction philosophies of the builders. Not every builder is convinced of the benefits of using a frame jig. Many builders believe that the jig can create inborn stresses that result as the tubing cools.

There are two other basic methods of brazing the frame—with *pins* or with *tack brazing*. Usually builders who braze with pins believe that it is the only acceptable way to build a frame and those that tack-braze believe it's the only acceptable way. Most builders tack or pin the tubes inside the lugs, recheck angles and alignment and, if everything is acceptable, complete the brazing of the frame. Each method accomplishes the same goal which is to temporarily attach the tube to the lug in such a way that if the alignment has been affected, the entire joint does not have to be dismantled. Individual preferences will be discussed in the chapters dealing with each builder. The frame builder must check to see that his pinning or tacking has not caused any stresses. He must learn to apply exactly the amount of heat that is required for

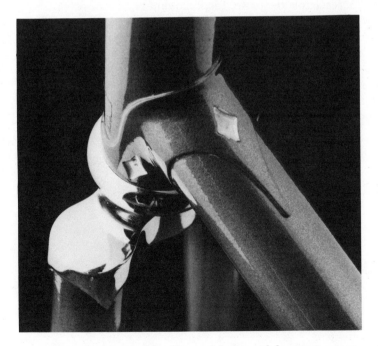

Figure 1-6: Simple diamond-shaped lug cutout on a Pogliaghi track bicycle.

the brazing rod that is being used. Lack of attention during the critical brazing process can totally nullify the benefits of good tubing and good lugs.

One feature of a custom frame that has been thought of as primarily cosmetic in nature is the *lug cutout* (figure 1–6). Many builders believe that, in addition to reduced weight, the cutouts provide a "window" to see how the braze is flowing during the brazing operation. Some builders believe that the cutout reduces surface tensions that occur during the brazing process.

Forks

Like the main triangle, the *forks* and stays involve several different designs and construction procedures. The fork is an interesting and complex part of the bicycle since it is the prime contributor to how the bicycle will handle. It consists of the fork tips, blades, reinforcing tangs, crown, and steering column. Its shape can increase or decrease responsiveness, comfort, and safety. Most quality builders use Campagnolo fork tips. However, there are many others (Shimano Dura-Ace, Sun Tour, Simplex, Huret) that are satisfactory. The *fork blades* and steering columns are produced by the major tube manufacturers and the *fork crowns* are usually produced by the major lug manufacturers.

There are three types of construction for fork crowns— *pressed* steel (stamped), *forged*, and *cast*. Pressed crowns are

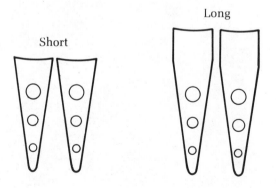

Long

Short

Figure 1-7: Detail: reinforcing tang (see figure 1-1).

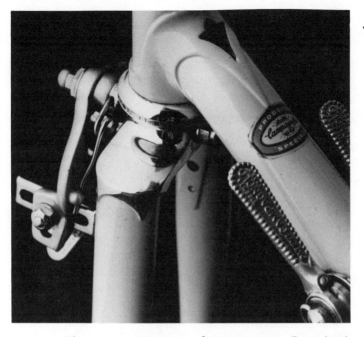

Figure 1-8: More complex cutout on a Guerciotti road bicycle.

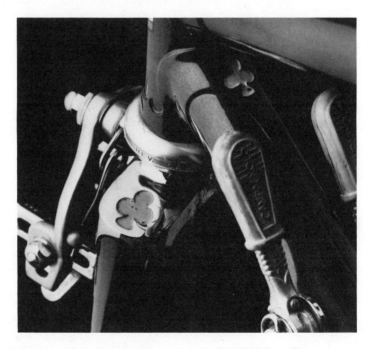

Figure 1-9: This cutout is so famous that it immediately identifies the builder as Ernesto Colnago. In this case, the clover leaf also appears on the semi-sloping fork crown.

usually found on inexpensive production bicycles although there are certain custom frame builders who prefer the pressed crowns. They are the weakest of the three crowns. In general, quality frame builders depend on forged or cast crowns according to the use of the bicycle. Like a forged hand tool, the forged crown is produced with the grain of the steel "in line." They are very strong but they require a great deal of filing to properly clean their pitted finish. Like cast lugs, the cast crown is extremely expensive, very strong, and usually comes with the greatest degree of accuracy in tolerances. There are three basic designs of fork crowns: *semi-sloping*, *fully sloping*, and the *flat* crown. Each has a number of advantages and disadvantages:

> Semi-sloping—The semi-sloping crown is becoming the most popular crown on custom frames. It is sometimes known as an *Italian section* because it is designed to fit the large section, 19-mm. oval blades that, until recently, have been available only in Columbus tubing. It is often preferred for *criterium*-type riding because it is light, very strong, and has great strength against the lateral pressures encountered in high-speed cornering.

Fully sloping

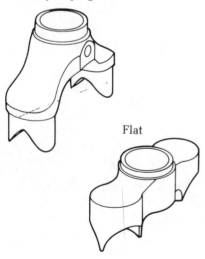

Flat

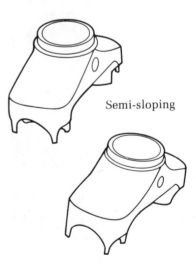

Semi-sloping

Figure 1-10: Fork crowns in cast steel.

Fully sloping—This fork crown is often referred to as the Italian sloping or the Cinelli crown because it had been developed originally by Cino Cinelli. It is the strongest fork crown available but it is also very heavy. There are many opposing opinions on the benefits of this type of crown. Its chief disadvantage is its weight. The fully sloping crown is considerably heavier than the flat or semi-sloping crowns. Furthermore, many people do not like it because it is so strong that a front-end collision will usually bend the frame tubes without any damage to the fork crown or, in many cases, the entire fork. Some riders would prefer replacing a bent fork since it is considerably less expensive than a new frame, however, Signore Cinelli believes that a fork should *never* break since the rider will be unable to control his bicycle in the event of a broken fork. Since a broken frame is usually ridable, it presents less of a safety hazard than a broken fork. Signore Cinelli's other rationale for the fully sloping design are covered in more detail in chapter 14.

Another controversy involving the fully sloping crown is its unique method of fork blade attachments. It is an integral crown and the fork blades fit *over* the crown. All other crowns fit over the fork blades. Some builders believe that the fully sloping crown is more difficult to use since it requires more careful fitting and brazing. There is an increased possibility of overheating the fork blades since the heat from the torch must pass through the fork blades to reach the crown.

Flat—The flat crown is not quite as strong as the semi- and the fully sloping crowns. It has been very popular since it is strong enough for average use and it is the easiest crown for the builder to use. This crown is available in both road and track configurations.

Although the fork crown can contribute to the style of the bicycle and some increased rigidity, all of the three types of fork crowns are stronger than the fork blades that are attached. Most fork failures occur immediately below the fork crown and are a direct result of the effects of extended use of tubes that have become brittle from overheating, or they result from crash damage.

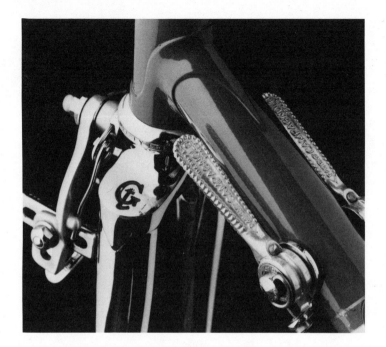

Figure 1-11: This microfusione (cast) fork crown carries the logo of its builder—Gios-Torino.

Fork blades also vary in design according to their use. Since a road bicycle is fitted with brakes, the fork blade must be oval to eliminate the shuddering which would otherwise result under hard braking. Track bicycles, which have no brakes, have round fork blades due to the greatly increased stresses caused by centrifugal force and *side-loading* caused by the banking of a track. Since tracks have a smooth surface, the necessity for a fork to act as a shock absorber is reduced.

Fork design has changed with the improvement in roads. Years ago, forks had a great deal of bend at the bottom which was necessary for adequate shock absorption. Racing bicycles of the fifties had more *rake* (bend) than the touring bicycles today. Current thinking in fork design is that as the radius of the bend in the fork is increased, the strength of the fork is also increased.

Chainstays and Seatstays

        Of all the parts of the frame, the *chainstays* seem to generate the smallest amount of controversy. Some builders prefer round chainstays, some prefer oval, and some prefer round with indentations for tires and chainwheels. Most builders do not believe that there is a significant difference in actual use. However, there are some differences noted in the method of attaching the *seatstays* to the seat lug. Many builders vary the method of attaching seatstays in response to the customer's request (which is often the result of "style"). Some (notably Cinelli) have firm beliefs in the advantages of a particular style. There are three basic styles: *fastback, semi-wrap,* and *wrapover* (or fully wrapped).

        Most builders agree that the fastback stay is the weakest of the three. It is primarily used on time trial or *pursuit* bicycles. The fastback stay is rarely used on touring bicycles since the seatstays attach to the back of the seat tube or seat lug and the clearance is

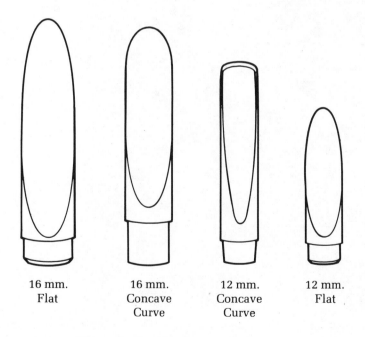

16 mm.	16 mm.	12 mm.	12 mm.
Flat	Concave	Concave	Flat
	Curve	Curve	

Figure 1-12: Seat lug top eyes.

Figure 1-13: Wrapover or fully wrapped seatstay. This style of stay attachment is primarily popular with the British builders. It is strong but heavier than the semi-wrap or most fastbacks.

Figure 1-14: The semi-wrap stay can be made in two ways. It can be chamfered with a plate brazed over the opening, or it can be a plug such as ones sold by the lug manufacturers. Guerciotti uses the flat surface to personalize his frames.

too narrow to permit room for fenders and *clincher* tires. The chief advantage of this stay is its light weight and clean appearance.

The semi-wrap seatstay attaches to the side of the seat lug. Some builders prefer to chamfer the stay and braze a top plate to fill the hollow section. Others cut off the stay near the top and install a plug. The semi-wrap is usually considered to be the strongest type of seat cluster.

Figure 1-15: This semi-wrap style is usually accomplished with a "plug." This is a 12-mm. stay such as found on a 49-cm. Colnago road frame.

The wrapover seatstay is strong but has the disadvantage of being the heaviest means of attaching the seatstays. The actual attachment of the seatstays is accomplished like the semi-wrap, except the two ends are connected by filling the space with braze. The wrapover is then filed to achieve its smooth lines. This design is seen primarily on frames of British manufacturers.

Figure 1-16: Note the beefy-looking, 16-mm. semi-wrap stay used on this 58-cm. track bicycle. Pogliaghi (see chapter 16) adds a personal touch to his bicycles with a transfer of his signature on the top tube.

Figure 1-17: A completely different variation of the semi-wrap stay. This is a chamfered stay which has a curved top plate brazed over the opening.

Unlike most builders, Cinelli believes that the seat lug is extremely important. All Cinelli frames come with a unique *cast seat lug* that is far stronger than any other seat lug. Since most builders do not believe that the additional strength is necessary, they do not use the cast seat lug because of its additional weight. When we discussed his reasons for using the cast seat lug, Cinelli advised us that the additional strength was only one factor in the decision. Another essential factor is reduced wind resistance caused by the location of the seatstays *behind* the seat tube!

Now that we have reviewed the basic construction and building philosophy of a quality lightweight frame, let's take a

Figure 1-18: This is the unique Cinelli cast seat lug. Signore Cinelli believes it is superior to every other seat lug because its casting is stronger than the pressed lug, its stay attachment is perfectly centered at the same height as the center line of the top tube, and its rear mounting is unequaled for aerodynamic efficiency.

Figure 1-19: Fastback seatstay. This style is preferred by many time trialists because it gives the appearance of being light. In reality, it can be heavier than the semi-wrap stay because large amounts of metal are needed for the seat lug to attach the seatstays near the seat binder bolt.

look at some ways to determine if the frame is "well built." The use of special tools for measuring and testing the frame is covered in chapter 3.

Frame Checks You Can Perform

1. Examine overall finish of the frame. Are there gaps between the lugs and the tubes? Gaps indicate that the builder did not totally fill the space between the tube and the lug with braze. It can be an indicator that the emphasis during the building process was placed on quantity not quality. The size of

Figure 1-20: A lugless frame—a method of attaching the head tube to the down tube and top tube is called bronze welding or fillet brazing.

the gap is particularly important if the frame has been silver-brazed, since the strength of the joint is drastically reduced if the gap is over .003 inch. Is the brazing around the lugs well done? Around the fork tips? Are there signs of file marks? File marks are another indicator that the builder was in a hurry; however, they should only be used as an indicator. French builders, in particular, do not believe that the finish of the frame is as important as the care given to assembly. American builders, on the other hand, often file the lug to paper-thin proportions—a practice that most expert builders regard as a poor practice.

2. Check fork tips to see if the inside (where the axle goes) has been machined or filed. Sometimes a builder who is trying to hide unequal length stays or fork blades will increase the depth of opening of one fork tip to obtain proper alignment.

3. Are the threads clean in the bottom bracket? Most builders will take the time to clean up the threads after they have finished building the frame. Install the *bottom bracket cups* to check if the bottom bracket has been *faced* (cut off squarely). If the bottom bracket has not been faced, you will have to do it yourself, which requires expensive special tools, or pay a good bicycle shop to do it for you. As the cups are being screwed in, check to see if the bottom bracket is round or egg shaped. Unfortunately, the bottom bracket can become distorted and there is no way to fix an egg-shaped bottom bracket without replacing it!

4. Are the tubes mitered in the bottom bracket? The degree of care in the mitering can be seen only in the bottom bracket. By sticking your finger inside the tube you can also determine whether the builder used pins to keep the frame aligned while he was brazing.

5. Stick your finger inside the bottom bracket and the *seat tube*. If the tubes have been overheated it may be possible to feel slight distortions. Also, if the bicycle is not built with seamless tubing you may, in some cases, be able to feel the seam.

6. With *one* hand, squeeze the rear *dropouts* and then the fork ends. After performing this test on several different bicycles, it becomes a relatively reliable means of determining the "stiffness" of the frame.

Remember, however, that stiffness in itself does not guarantee a good frame.

Most of the time, purchasing a bicycle frame from a reputable builder will eliminate buying a "bad" bicycle. Sometimes a good-looking frame can be an absolute disaster, however. One example that demonstrates this is a situation we experienced while operating our bicycle shop. One of our club riders won a frame in a race and we initially agreed to sell it for him through the store. Unfortunately, the rider had to practically pay someone to take the frameset because of all its problems. The rear end was bent over 1½ inches to the left and the bottom bracket was incorrectly tapped so that the fixed cup had to be inserted on the wrong side (English threads). The adjustable cup had to go behind the chainwheel! The front forks were so twisted that the forks had to be spread to install the front wheel. But the frame had a nice paint job.

To reduce the possibility of a purchase you will later regret, ask bicycle enthusiasts for their experiences with frames. There is one foolproof test of a frame—give it 10 years of hard use. Talk to people who own the type of frame you are interested in purchasing.

Now that we have reviewed basic frame design and components, let's take an in-depth look at the two most popular brands of tubing used in high-quality lightweight frames.

CHAPTER 2

Bicycle Tubing

The primary problem in describing bicycle tubing is that the differences between the available types of tubing are extremely subtle. They are primarily compositional. For instance, Reynolds, a major manufacturer of bicycle tubing, has decided to use a small amount of manganese in their tubing which subtly alters its characteristics. The primary change in the tubing as a result of the addition of manganese is realized in the actual frame-brazing process rather than a difference in the ride characteristics of the frame. Columbus, another major manufacturer of bicycle tubing, adds chrome to their tubing. Again, this slightly varied tubing composition does not result in noticeably different ride characteristics as much as it changes the type of brazing methods that should be used on the frame.

If the average bicycle rider cannot readily tell the difference in tubing, then why is bicycle tubing such an important factor in the choice of a top-quality bicycle? There are two primary answers.

One, to make a butted bicycle tube (the "butting" process is explained in detail in this chapter) is extremely difficult and requires far greater production costs than a *standard drawn* (or *plain gauge*) tube. Although the butted tube only provides marginally different specifications from the standard tube, the strength characteristics for the weight of the tube are important enough to the serious cyclist to justify the greatly increased cost. It is important, therefore, for the consumer to be able to identify the type of tubing in a bicycle to insure that he or she is getting the proper tubing for the price.

Two, a high-quality *double-butted* tube that has been properly brazed has a considerably longer life and will retain its strength for a far greater period of time than an inexpensive tube that has been improperly brazed. This is one important reason why so many people are interested in *custom frames*. The key to understanding tubing is to understand the processes that the builder uses when he is actually building a frame. One of the most important aspects of frame design is matching the proper brazing techniques and design with the appropriate bicycle tubing.

Are there any real differences between the varying brands of bicycle tubes? One very obvious difference is the design variance that exists between individual tubing manufacturers. For instance, Columbus pioneered the Italian section fork blade which provided vastly improved handling characteristics of the bicycle. Other than specific design variations like fork blades and availability in certain *gauges*, the basic frame tubes are very similar in their ability to perform.

Why are only two tubing manufacturers, Reynolds and Columbus, included in the following pages? The decision had been based on the fact that the vast majority of all highly respected master frame builders use either Reynolds or Columbus tubing. Although there are other tubes made in France, Japan, and in the United States, for several reasons Columbus and Reynolds remain the two top choices of the master frame builders.

First, there is a great deal of history that supports the popularity of the two large tubing manufacturers. Both were pioneers in the research and development of the modern-day bicycle tube. Simply, they started before anyone else did and they came up with lasting and successful designs. It should also be obvious that the majority of the most famous frame builders in the world are located in close proximity to the major tubing manufacturers. As the reputations of the builders grew, so did the reputations of the tubing manufacturers. Another factor that greatly contributed to the continued popularity of the two tubing manufacturers, is the tendency for builders to have little desire to try alternative brands of tubing. The two popular tubings are of sufficiently high quality to virtually eliminate the desire of any builder to try other products.

Only recently, as a result of the bicycle boom, has any experimentation in using other tubing occurred. This resulted from the inability of the tubing manufacturers to increase production as fast as sales demanded. Why haven't other tubing manufacturers become involved in the marketing of high-quality bicycle tubing? The reason is primarily due to the incredibly large investment in heavy machinery that is required. The world's bicycle market is very small when compared to the potential steel use for other industries such as the automobile or the construction industry. Without the large market potential and subsequent large sales volume, it simply isn't worth the manufacturers' investment in the heavy machinery and development costs that would be required.

Because of the nature of this chapter with its highly technical content, the casual reader is advised to skip to chapter 3 describing Campagnolo bicycle components and the use of their special tools. For those persons interested in the technical side of bicycle frames, the rest of the chapter provides both a history of the two major companies and technical information regarding the composition and working requirements of the bicycle tubes.

TI Reynolds

In the 1880s, Mr. Alfred Milward Reynolds was obsessed with making lightweight bicycle tubing, but met failure after failure when the tube continually buckled at the ends. In an effort to obtain the necessary strength, he fitted slightly smaller-size tubes at the ends of the tubing to serve as reinforcing liners. Although the liners provided the necessary strength, Reynolds felt that additional tubing was an unnecessary additional weight.

In 1887 he invented the process he called *butting*, patented the process and founded the Patented Butted Tube Company in 1898. At that time, only bicycle tubing was manufactured. Everyone recognized the benefits of the butted process and, after the patent expired, other tubing companies started to use the process. The following is an explanation of the butting process provided by TI Reynolds:

> For lightweight machines, whether for touring or racing, a "cold drawn seamless" tube is required—one which starts life as a solid ingot which is pierced hot, either in a hydraulic press, or by running it between inclined rollers which force it over a pointed mandrel, thus "pushing the hole through the bar." Further hot-rolling results in a "hollow" or "bloom," already looking like a tube, which goes to the seamless tube manufacturer to be cold drawn down to the diameter and gauge required for our cycle frames.

At every stage, each bloom is annealed (i.e., softened by heating), and pickled in acid to remove scale. Then one end is reduced to a smaller diameter, known as the "tag," to enable it to pass through the drawing die. After lubricating with a special compound of oil, soft soap, and other ingredients, it is ready for drawing. Drawbenches come in a variety of sizes, some being mighty monsters over a hundred feet long, with the die-plate nearly halfway along.

The bloom is slipped over a shaped plug on a long mandrel bar, fixed to the end of the drawbench, the tag is pushed through the die and gripped relentlessly by serrated steel jaws, known in the tube trade as "dogs." These are mounted on a "wagon," running on a track containing a large continuous multiple roller chain, to which the wagon is automatically locked when the dogs have gripped the tag, thus drawing the tube through the die, and over the plug on the end of its mandrel. As this has moved to a position within the die, the metal is in effect squeezed between the die and the plug, thus reducing both diameter and thickness, and at the same time increasing the length. Several such "passes," interspersed with annealing and pickling operations, are necessary before the tube is the right diameter and gauge, accurate to within three-thousandths of an inch, for the manufacture of frame tubes, forks, and stays for your new bicycle.

In 1923, the name of the company was changed to the Reynolds Tube Company, Limited. The cycling tubing at this time had been called "HM" and was of high manganese content and low molybdenum content. A major change occurred in 1935 when 531DB tubing was developed. Reynolds always points out that 531 is said as "five-three-one" not five hundred thirty-one or five thirty-one. Reynolds 531 is a manganese-molybdenum tubing— the 531 refers to the ratio of the major elements it contains. The people at Reynolds are also quick to point out that unlike the advertisements of some bicycle companies, Reynolds 531 is not chrome molybdenum. Reynolds believe that their manganese-molybdenum tubes have greater ductility than chrome molybdenum tubes and, consequently, they will retain a greater per-

Figure 2-2: The machine that "butts" the tube.

Figure 2-1: The machine at TI Reynolds that actually makes the tubes. Three tubes are drawn simultaneously (at the top). One end is reduced to a smaller diameter and pulled through the drawing die and over the shaped mandrel. The tube is pressed through this process several times before the final diameter and gauge are reached. The three tubes visible at the bottom are in an intermediate stage of completion.

Figure 2-3: This method of tapering stays and fork blades is seldom used now. TI Reynolds found it difficult to locate and train persons with the necessary "touch" to feed the tubing to the machine by hand. Consequently, the process is now handled entirely by machine.

Figure 2-4: No machine has been developed to bend fork blades with more accuracy and care than this workman. All fork blades are raked by hand!

centage of their strength after brazing. While there is some chrome in the tubing to effect the proper physical properties, it is in substantially smaller quantities than would qualify it to be called chrome molybdenum tubing.

As road surfaces continued to improve, and the reliability of the tubing remained unchallenged, Reynolds developed a new lighter gauge called Reynolds 531SL (Special Lightweight).

A major change occurred in 1975, when the new 753 tubing was introduced. In spite of reduced wall thickness (it's only .3 mm.) and lighter weight, the new tubing is 50 percent stronger than 531!

The 753 tubing is very special tubing that has not been made generally available yet. Because of the special nature of the tubing, only pre-evaluated builders will be able to buy 753. Reynolds has distributed two sets of the tubing to some "master" builders for assembly in a test frame. The frame must be sent to Reynolds for destruction testing. If, and only if, the frame has been correctly brazed, 753 will be available to those builders. The tubing requires extremely close tolerances since the only approved method of brazing is with silver.

In the United Kingdom, only Bob Jackson, Harry Quinn, and TI Raleigh have received approval to build with 753. In the United States, Proteus Design (the only U.S. Reynolds agent) had built a 753 frame and sent it to England for evaluation. In turn, Proteus Design has been approved to build with Reynolds 753. To give you an idea how light the tubing is, let's look at the approximate frameset weight of bicycles built with 531DB, 531SL, and 753.

Weights of frame with fork, seatstays, and chainstays:

> 531DB—5½ lbs. (2.5 kg.)
> 531SL—5 lbs. (2.3 kg.)
> 753—4 lbs. (1.8 kg.)

In 1977, the Reynolds Tube Company, Limited changed their name to TI Reynolds because they make more than just bicycle tubes. The bicycle tubing division is only one of the three divisions in the continually growing company. One division manufactures the *flash welded* rims for the Rolls Royce Olympic engine used in the Concorde and another division manufactures hydraulic cylinders. The tubing division provided frame tubing for the now-defunct Jaguar XKE and they still make tubing for wheelchairs.

For the technically inclined, we have included the following information, provided by Reynolds, that details their unique fork blade construction. Recommended brazing procedures are found in Appendix III.

Figure 2-5: Any of these Reynolds 531 transfers signify that the bicycle has been built with Reynolds tubing but the differences should be noted. The first three indicate that the frame has butted frame tubes, seatstays, and chainstays, and taper gauge fork blades. The following two indicate that the frame has been built with Reynolds 531 butted frame tubes but that the chainstays and fork blades used are from another manufacturer. The last decal denotes that the frame has been built with plain gauge Reynolds 531 frame tubes plus 531 fork blades and chainstays.

30

Fork Blade Construction

Tapering a tube for a fork blade, chainstay, or seatstay, is a highly skilled task. Two steel rollers, one above the other, rotate so that the faces in contact with each other are moving towards the operator. In those faces are semi-circular grooves, matched to present a round hole, which progressively diminishes as the rollers rotate, then suddenly opens out to full diameter again. The full diameter is that of the tube to be tapered, and the length of the tapered groove in the rollers coincides with the required length of tapered tube.

As the full diameter faces the operator, he quickly pushes in the tube as far as he can. The rollers push it out again, but squeeze a little into the tapered groove. As the full diameter comes round, so the tube is pushed in again, going in a little further on account of the small length already reduced in diameter. This is further reduced as the tube is pushed out again. The operation is repeated at the rate of about sixty strokes a minute until the tube reaches a pre-set stop behind the rollers. All the time, while the tube is being pushed in and out, the operator is rotating it, to ensure that its soundness is maintained. A stay takes between a quarter and half a minute, according to length, and is afterwards trued up for straightness.

Fork blades are made this way, from round tubing, which is afterwards shaped to oval or D at the larger end if required. They are then bent round a former in a simple hand-operated bender. The tool looks almost primitive, but is very effective and accurate.

Modern road surfaces are generally good—but even so, if our front forks were rigid we would have a very uncomfortable ride, and use up so much energy absorbing the vibration in our arms that mileages would tumble and times would stretch alarmingly. So the front fork blades are curved to a carefully planned "rake" to provide resilience and so smooth out some of the road-roughness.

This is where Problem No. 1 crops up. The weakest

point in a cycle tube is adjacent to the brazed joint, so we need the top of the fork blade to be rigid. Now Problem No. 2. When a tube is tapered, quite naturally its walls tend to thicken up as the diameter decreases. So now we have a typical fork blade, where the top is of adequate thickness for rigidity, but the bottom is thicker than the top, thus partially defeating the effect of the rake, and killing some of the resilience!

What can be done about this? Some cycle manufacturers use a lighter gauge fork blade to get the resilience, and put a liner in the top for rigidity, but by far the best solution is the taper gauge fork. You will remember how Mr. Reynolds invented the Butting process, whereby the wall thickness of a tube could be increased at one or both ends without affecting the outside diameter. You will also probably remember that a fork blade starts life as a straight parallel tube. We take a light gauge tube of the right diameter, put in a single butt with a long gradual change of gauge, and then taper the end with the thinner gauge. Bent to shape, we have the Reynolds Taper Gauge fork blade, with a wall thickness less at the resilient end than at the rigid end. The result is that road shocks are smoothed, and more energy can be devoted to making the wheels go round, farther, faster, or with less fatigue.

A. L. Colombo

Angelo Luigi Colombo started manufacturing tubing in 1924 for the aircraft industry. The production of double-butted bicycle tubing began in 1930. Signore Colombo is now 86 years old but still comes to work two or three times each week. His son, Antonio, is the director of the company which has become, with TI Reynolds, one of the most sought-after tubes for lightweight bicycles.

It is interesting that the engineers at Columbus feel very differently about chrome vs. manganese than those at Reynolds. For instance, the only tube in the Columbus line that is carbon manganese is the "inexpensive" set. All of the top-of-the-line tubing is chrome molybdenum. The design intent at Columbus is high strength and high elongation since low elongation tends toward brittleness. Furthermore, they will *not* build tubes with less than .5-mm. wall thickness. They believe that oxidation during the brazing process can reduce the effective thickness of the tube by as much as .1 mm. They seem consistent in their beliefs, since even their "record" extra-light tubing is .5 mm. thick.

The specialties at Columbus are their fork blades and fork columns. Unlike TI Reynolds, they do not believe that a taper gauge fork is desirable. The Columbus fork is identified by its smooth curve and large section. This design responds to the

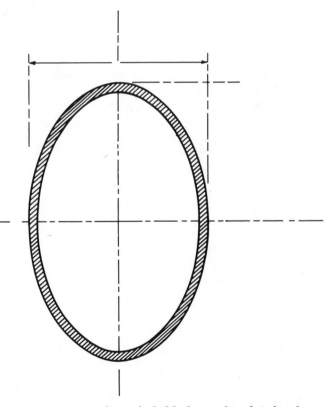

Figure 2-6: Cross-section outline, fork blade made of Columbus tubing. The diameter and wall thickness are kept proportionate to the bending stress throughout its length. Note that the ellipse of the fork blade has an equal thickness.

Figure 2-7: Cutaway, Columbus fork column section.

cyclist's need for strength while cornering without adverse amounts of road shock over bumps. The fork column is also unique with its two thicknesses and five helical ribs (similar to rifling in a gun barrel) designed to withstand enormous torsional forces without excessive weight (figure 2–7).

As a result of the enormous popularity of the Columbus blades (they became known as Italian section forks), TI Reynolds has recently marketed blades of similar design. Since many of the English builders used Reynolds tubing on their frames, they had been unable to offer the Italian section forks. They now report that a very high percentage of their frames are built using the Reynolds Italian section forks. Many riders suggest that the Italian section forks do provide a considerably more comfortable ride and, at the same time, improved cornering power.

A new seatstay is offered by Columbus, and although it has not gained any popularity in this country, some Italian builders claim that it is extremely popular on the Continent. This stay has its largest outside diameter in the center of the tube. That is, the tube has a narrow section near the seat lug, increases to its maximum halfway down the stay, and then decreases to the same size section as the top where it is brazed to the fork end. There are no additional advantages to the stay; it is produced for "aesthetic" appeal.

Now that we have reviewed the properties of the two major brands of bicycle tubes, the components that hold them together, and the elements of design that contribute to a good handling and strong bicycle, let's take a look at the steps that must be completed before the frame is ready for assembly. Since these steps require special tools, we have included a step-by-step guide to explain their use. The next chapter covers the history of the manufacturer of these tools—S.P.A. Brevetti Internazionali Campagnolo—the world's most famous name in bicycle components.

CHAPTER 3
Tools for Frame Building

S.P.A. Brevetti Internazionali
Campagnolo
36100 Vicenza
Italia

The name Campagnolo has become associated with the finest bicycle parts available in the world today. It is extremely rare to find a professional bicycle racer who does not ride a bicycle that is completely Campagnolo equipped, unless he is compelled to ride other equipment because of national regulations or he is sponsored by a competitor of Campagnolo.

Campagnolo has maintained its reputation because of the uniformly high-quality components that have a low failure rate. Furthermore, even the smaller replacement parts are generally available, unlike many of its competitors. Before we look at some of the reasons why Campagnolo distinguishes itself, let's review the events that led to the founding of the company.

Tullio Campagnolo was an enthusiastic racer who participated in hundreds of races between 1922 and 1930. Although he did not win any of the major classics, he did participate in races as important as the Milan–San Remo and the Giro della Lombardia. During a particularly brutal race held in freezing temperatures in conjunction with the Feast of San Martino, Tullio Campagnolo punctured in mid race. As the pack sped by, he attempted to loosen the bicycle's frozen wing nuts to replace the tire. His frozen fingers, numb and insensitive from the cold, were unable to loosen the wing nuts that had become clogged with snow and ice. He watched in vain as the pack rode by.

Instead of accepting the technical limitations of the hubs with wing nut attachments, Campagnolo resolved that he would create an alternative means of attaching the wheels that would operate efficiently under all conditions. The outcome of his unfortunate experience in the snow has remained as the lightest, most effective method of wheel attachment to this day: the *quick-release hub* mechanism.

Motivated by the successful operation of the quick-release hub, Campagnolo began examining other bicycle parts for their shortcomings. He completed his first gear-changing mechanism in 1930, although it did not reach its final form until 1933. Soon the mechanism began to appear on some of the bicycles of the top professional riders. It was a complex affair that involved two control levers. The first lever released the rear spindle and the second lever controlled the gear change that occurred only when the rider would pedal backwards.

The next derailleur to appear was called the Paris Roubaix and was essentially the same, except it was controlled by one lever. This system was incredibly complex since one movement of the lever loosened the spindle release mechanism, changed gears, and tightened the spindle after the gear change was completed! It is interesting to note that this mechanism, unlike today's derailleur, did not utilize two pulleys for chain tension—the chain was adjusted as an integral part of the gear change!

The Italian bicycle factories became the first manufacturers to include Campagnolo equipment on their racing bicycles. Accordingly, Campagnolo has played an important part in the development of the feeling that the Italians have been the primary source of bicycle innovation.

Not content to leave his design unchanged, in 1951, Campagnolo developed the variable parallelogram derailleur as we know it today. It was designated the Gran Sport. It was soon replaced with the brass Record derailleur and later became the alloy Nuovo Record.

Campagnolo's recent use of ultralightweight (and ultraexpensive) titanium alloys has resulted in a new derailleur known as the Super Record. The operation of the Super Record and the Nuovo Record are the same—except for differences in the weight of the components.

Since the development of the quick-release axle, Campagnolo has developed over 180 other inventions. It is important to recognize that, unlike many inventors who started innovative products, Campagnolo took a new idea and developed it until it would be totally reliable and without equal. Many times his desire for near-perfect quality control resulted in prices that were far above competitive products. In spite of the high prices people lined up to purchase his products for one basic reason: They worked better than anything else available. Campagnolo products became so well known that people were willing to buy equipment that had been manufactured by competitors who, for all practical purposes, copied some of Campagnolo's designs. Although the copies were usually substantially less expensive to purchase, Campagnolo's sales remained high because of their undisputed quality. Today, S.P.A. Brevetti Internazionali Campagnolo has been selected as the technical assistant for all world championship and Olympic cycling events.

What contributes to Campagnolo's high reputation and legendary quality? Most important is the hidden engineering. Campagnolo uses its direct communications line with professional cyclists as a source for ideas. If a problem is recognized in the "field," the engineers at Campagnolo respond with designs to eliminate or reduce the problem. Although the appearance of the product may be unchanged (or externally appears the same as a competitor's product) examination "under the surface" would reveal important features. For instance:

- Campagnolo became famous for the wear characteristics of its alloy chainrings. The teeth in Campagnolo chainrings are gear-cut, while some manufacturers utilize less expensive methods which, when combined with softer alloys, do not allow long life.

- The Campagnolo bottom bracket axle is designed to repel water from the bearings as it revolves during normal pedaling.

- The Campagnolo hand brake lever handlebar attachment bolt passes through the body of the lever instead of the pivot pin. Unlike most designs, this greatly reduces the pressure to the pivot pin and results in a brake that operates smoothly under all conditions and a lever that is less prone to failure.

- The quick-release lever on the Campagnolo brake allows for varying degrees of adjustment. The quick-release lever on most brakes is fully "open" or completely "closed." The Campagnolo quick-release brake lever allows the rider to compensate for a damaged rim (caused by a pothole or crash) by opening the brake shoes to the point where they clear the out-of-true portion of the rim.

In addition to a complete line of bicycle parts, Campagnolo produces components for motorcycles, airplanes, helicopters, sounding balloons, and satellites. They also produce some unique consumer items like an enormous corkscrew and a nutcracker that is designed to crack the hull of the nut without damaging the meat! We were also told that Campagnolo has designed an improved pants hanger although there are no current plans for production.

The remainder of this chapter is devoted to an explanation of

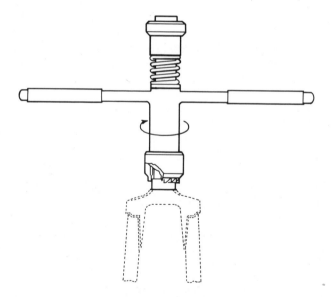

Figure 3-1: Crown bearing race. The crown race cutter (Campagnolo tool #718) is fitted over the steering tube to accurately cut the lower bearing race. A tension spring maintains adequate pressure to evenly cut the required surface.

the use of the more complicated Campagnolo special tools. We have included this because the understanding of the operation of the tools clarifies operations that are essential in the construction of a quality bicycle frame.

Armed with a knowledge of the basic frame components, let's examine the opinions of the experts at Campagnolo on how to properly join the materials into a machine that will contribute to the rider's assets and reduce the rider's weaknesses.

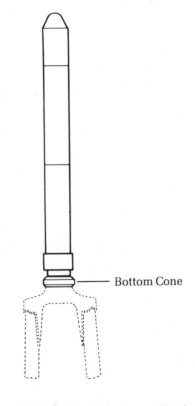

Bottom Cone

Figure 3-2: Installation of lower bearing cone. The headset cup punch (tool #722) is used to install the lower bearing cone after the bearing race has been cut.

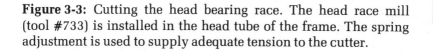

Figure 3-3: Cutting the head bearing race. The head race mill (tool #733) is installed in the head tube of the frame. The spring adjustment is used to supply adequate tension to the cutter.

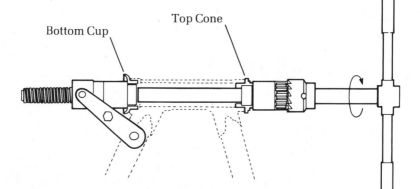

Bottom Cup   Top Cone

Figure 3-4: Mounting the bearing cups to the head tube. Tool #733 is used in conjunction with fitted sleeves (tool #728) to press fit the bearing cups into the head tubes. This tool reduces the possibility of cracking or distorting the head tube when hammering the cups into position. The cutting action performed in figure 3-3 insures a perfect 90-degree angle cut and the installation step (with the use of tool #728) insures perfect cup alignment.

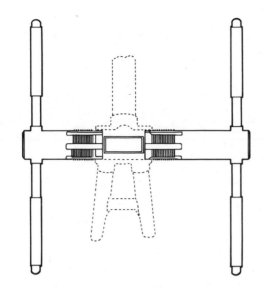

Figure 3-5: Cutting the bottom bracket threads. Perfectly concentric threads require a tool that will cut threads in both sides of the bottom bracket in perfect alignment (tool #721). Different-size taps are available to accommodate the popular thread specifications. Since the taps rotate on the same center axis, perfect alignment will result.

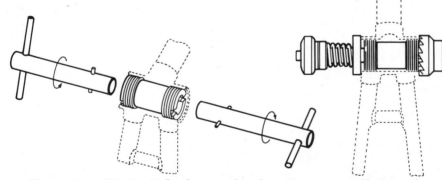

Figure 3-6: "Facing" the bottom bracket. Proper installation of the bottom bracket cups cannot be guaranteed without accurate facing of the bottom bracket. The bottom bracket face cutter (tool #725) is a fairly complex unit which includes an internal guide sleeve that is fitted into the bottom bracket. The bottom bracket face cutter is fitted into the sleeve, which insures a perfectly aligned "face" for the bearing cups.

41

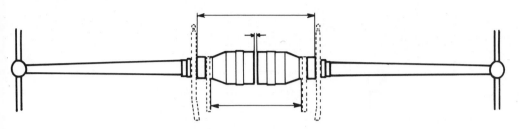

Figure 3-7: Alignment of front and rear fork tips. The Campagnolo special tool for fork tip alignment (tool #H) is used to correct wheel installation (or removal) problems. The front fork is checked by moving the adjustable washers to their outside position and inserting each side of the tool into the fork tip. If the tips are properly aligned, the machined faces of the tool will be exactly 1 mm. apart along the entire face of the tool. The same method of checking the tips is used on the rear, however, the washers are set to their inside position.

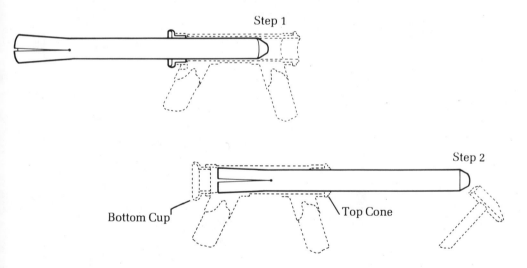

Step 1

Step 2

Bottom Cup

Top Cone

Figure 3-8: Removal of headset bearing cups. The headset cup remover (tool #723) is used to remove the cups without damage. The tool is inserted at the smallest point until its expanding section is located adjacent to the cup to be removed. The head of the tool is gently tapped to remove the cup with minimum stress on the head tube.

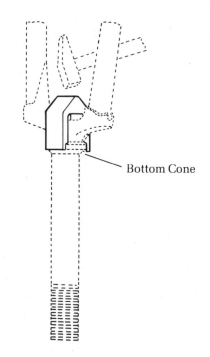

Bottom Cone

Figure 3-9: Removal of bearing cone from fork. The fork crown race remover (tool #729) is installed on the underside of the fork crown with its projected tips resting on the bearing cone. Gently tapping the head of the tool will force the cone from the fork without damage.

To isolate and clarify each builder's beliefs, the following chapters are devoted to individual frame builders. The chapters are grouped by the nationality of the builder and each builder is presented in alphabetical order within the group.

PART II
British
Frame Builders

The British seem to have the largest ratio of frame builders per capita in the world due to the strong demand for their products. The huge American market is the primary reason for continuous growth in the British cycling industry. Consequently, the demand for custom frames in the United States has, at times, outstripped supply.

British frames are best known for their unique baked-on finish which is called *stove enamelling*. This method involves a multistep paint process that necessitates "stoving" after each application of paint. Stove enamelling has become synonymous with British frames even though each individual builder performs his own variation on the number of coats required and baking times.

England is also the home of Reynolds tubing, one of the most popular tubes used in quality frames in the world (see chapter 2). The proximity of the TI Reynolds factory has contributed to the development of English frame builders by providing easy access to frame-building materials and advice. The diameter of the tubing developed by TI Reynolds for the British market is larger than the standard metric sizes developed for Europe.

Almost all British frame builders will build a frameset to suit a rider's individual physique and riding needs. In many cases, the British masters work very closely with individual riders to insure the best possible fit. Most of the English frame builders have raced (time trialing usually) and have an excellent understanding of all phases of cycling. Of all the European builders, the British frame builders are most sympathetic to the needs of the tourist. They will build a frameset for a tourist just as readily as for a racer. Some builders such as the Taylors go one step further by constructing their own specialized touring racks to precisely fit special makes of *panniers*.

Wraparound and fastback seatstays are generally found only on British framesets. If you are interested in ornate, handcut lugs, you should look to the British builders since they are the only ones, as a group, willing to take the extra time to create personalized "one-of-a-kind" lugwork.

CHAPTER 4

Condor Cycles

Condor Cycles
90-94 Grays Inn Road
London WCIX 8AA
England

The Condor motto is Our Claim to Fame Is in the Name. It is an appropriate motto, for Condor frames are generally regarded as some of the best of the English frames.

Condor Cycles is located in the west central section of London, just down the street from the famous Dickens' House, where Charles Dickens lived from 1837–39. Although Grays Inn Road is a typically busy London street, it seems that the majority of the traffic stops at Condor Cycles, especially during the lunch hour. Consequently, if you arrive between two and three o'clock in the afternoon, you might as well go to see the collection of books and illustrations displayed at Dickens' House since the people at Condor Cycles usually lock the door after the lunch hour rush to have lunch themselves. If you're not a museum buff, you might want to join the people congregated outside the door of the bicycle shop, waiting for it to reopen. It's not hard to find someone who will tell you why they think that buying from Condor is worth the wait.

Background

Once inside the small store, you will be amazed at all the merchandise. It is packed to the ceiling with parts, accessories, frames, bicycles, and clothing. There are doors that open into closets and rooms that are filled with even more bicycle parts. In short, the place is too small for the amount of business that is being conducted. This is typical, however, of the better "enthusiast" stores that are found in England and on the Continent.

Monty Young is the owner and chief frame builder at Condor Cycles. Monty was 17 years old when he started manufacturing bicycle frames under the Condor label in 1946. He became interested in bicycle frame building as a result of some racing he did in his youth. He told us that he had very little guidance as a frame builder, and that everything he knows about frames has been self-taught.

Although Monty Young quit racing soon after he went into the bicycle industry on a full-time basis, his interest in racing did not diminish. Monty has been team manager of four British world teams, has sponsored a complete team in the Tour de France, and has sponsored several six-day races in London.

Condor Cycles employs two frame builders (one is Monty), two filers, and two painters. The chrome-plating, like that of most other builders, is done away from the premises by a professional chrome shop.

One of the filers employed at Condor Cycles is Grant Young, Monty's 19-year-old son, who is following in his father's footsteps. Grant has been working in the shop for two years and only now is he allowed to do some building. Grant thinks it takes about four years to become a good builder if the process is closely supervised by a master. He also thinks it would take someone even longer if he did not have the guidance of an experienced builder.

Although Grant works full time in his father's frame shop, he does find time to ride his bicycle. He competes as an amateur primarily in road racing events.

Building Philosophy

Today all the lugs used at Condor Cycles are stamped steel. They generally use lugs made by Haden, Roto, and Agrati. Years ago, they used cast lugs. However, they don't use them anymore because when they were sandblasted they tended to perforate and become brittle.

Monty Young uses all three styles of fork crowns: flat, semi-sloping, and fully sloping. The fully sloping integral Cinelli crown has been very popular for the last five years with Monty, but more and more customers are starting to request the cast

Figure 4-1: Wheel building at Condor.

semi-sloping crown. Monty thinks that both are very good and tries to match the style of the fork crown to the style of the lugs. On the lugless Barrachi model, he uses a fully sloping crown which is very pleasing since it is an extension of the clean lines maintained on the lugless frame. When using his handcut lugs on a frame, Monty will use a semi-sloping crown made by Haden because he can have a small design cut out on each side of the crown to match a similar effect on the lugs.

Two different sizes of seatstays are used. The 9/16 inch are used for smaller frames and the 5/8 inch are used on larger frames. Seat cluster arrangements vary but Condor never uses a fastback stay for a *racing frame*. Monty believes that track riding places the greatest strain on a frame and that the wrapover is the strongest seat cluster. The fastback is not used on Condor *touring frames* either since the English believe that all touring bicycles require 27-inch clincher tires with fenders. Therefore, it is not possible to fit this configuration within the reduced space created by a fastback stay. If you are planning on using the metric size 700 c tires, you'll have no problem with using a fastback seat cluster.

All Condor frames are built on jigs. In his machine shop, Monty has built separate jigs for the forks, main triangle, and stays. Condors are brazed together with either bronze or silver depending on the weight of the tubing to be used in the frame. Bronze is used on the regular Reynolds 531DB frames. Generally, silver is used only on the lightest gauges of tubing like Reynolds 531SL because it flows a lot easier on light metals at a low temperature. Monty hopes to be building Reynolds 753 frames very soon and on these he will also be using silver braze.

Monty uses only Reynolds tubing for his frames. He has used Columbus for the Condor Sienna, but with the advent of Reynolds 753, he plans to redesign the Sienna to make it suitable for 753 construction. His preference for Reynolds is a result of the excellent working relationship he has with TI Reynolds and the convenience in dealing with a British firm.

Frame Selection

At Condor Cycles you can get a frame built to your individual specifications. They prefer that you send them the exact specifications for the frame you want built. If, however, you send them only your body measurements, they will build according to their rules of thumb. They require three measurements: inside leg measurement, torso length, and arm length. By subtracting 9 inches from the inseam, they arrive at a seat tube size. The torso length will indicate the size of the top tube.

Condor Cycles builds both racing and touring frames. Although their brochure indicates that all the frames are for racing, two of the frames (the Superbe and the Italia) can be adapted for touring. Unlike some builders who believe a racing frame should be smaller than a touring frame, Monty designs the same size bicycle for racing or touring. On the touring bicycle, he prefers a head and seat angle of 72 degrees for comfort. For road racing, he usually builds with a 73-degree head and seat angle. For track racing, he prefers a 74-degree parallel frame; but if you asked for a six-day frame, it would have a 75-degree seat, 73-degree head, and a very low bottom bracket. These angles would all change if the bicycle frame being built is smaller than 21 inches or larger than 22½ inches. The angles would all vary on the smaller and larger Condor frames according to fixed relationships that Monty has developed through the years.

In building frames, Monty believes that the top tube should be short to reduce the flex, or sway, in the frame. He also recommends that a track frame be made an inch smaller than a road frame. He does this so that the rider's power is concentrated over the front wheel which makes it easier to control the bicycle on the banking.

When you order a Condor touring frame, it will be designed with adequate clearance for clincher tires and minimum clearance for mudguards. They will build a touring frame with minimum clearance for tubular tires only if requested. The racing model will be built with minimum clearances for sew-up tires. If you want a dual-purpose frame for touring and racing, they will divide the distance between the two equally, so as to be able to accommodate both types of tires.

Unless you advise to the contrary, the touring frame will generally have a slightly longer fork rake and wheelbase than the racing model. Monty buys only straight fork blades and he rakes them himself so that he can provide whatever specifications you desire. If there is no specification for fork rake given, Monty will rake it according to what he feels would best suit the use of the frame.

When Monty first started building frames, handcut lugs were very popular. At that time he designed eight different models of

Figure 4-2: One final check on a finished frame.

handcut lugs. Since it is almost impossible to buy the blanks to handcut lugs, he now offers only one style of handcut lug. Monty uses Haden *blanks* to handcut the lugs for his Superbe model. He cuts all the lugs personally and it takes him one full day. The only reason he still does it, he advised us, is because it has become a Condor trademark.

Since their production is limited, Condors have not been imported very heavily into the United States and consequently little is known about them. In the United Kingdom, however, Condor frames are considered to be some of the finest. Their reputation has grown primarily as a result of their excellent workmanship.

CHAPTER 5

JRJ Cycles, Limited

Bob Jackson Cycles
JRJ Cycles, Limited
148 Harehill Lane
Leeds LS8 5BD
England

Although its official name is JRJ Cycles, Limited, the firm is better known as Bob Jackson Cycles. It is located in Leeds, a city of 490,000 in the northern half of England. Leeds has been the center of the wool industry in England since the Middle Ages. Today this Yorkshire city has a diversified industrial base which gives it an interesting mixture of modern and Victorian architecture. Amidst this architectural grandeur is a small, unobtrusive building on Harehill Lane which sells lightweight bicycles, parts, and accessories.

Upon entering this small store, you are surrounded by a large array of well-displayed Reynolds 531DB framesets, most of them bearing the Bob Jackson or Merlin labels. The display area in the store is small, but the merchandise is very well organized. Everything has been dusted and polished and sits neatly in place.

At the front right corner of the showroom is a door that marks the entrance to Bob Jackson's office. Here you'll find a tidy, well-lit room with two desks—one for Mr. Jackson and one for his administrative secretary. Behind the large desk where Bob Jackson sits is the door leading to the frame-building shop. On the wall behind Bob's desk hangs a picture of Jacques Pinto, an American bicycle distributor, with former U.S. President Gerald Ford. The picture is signed by Mr. Ford with a note of thanks for the bicycle that Bob Jackson had built for him.

Background

Bob Jackson bicycles gained popularity in the United States during the bicycle boom of the late 1960s through the early 1970s. His frames are beautifully finished and, during the bicycle boom, seemed to be more easily available than some of his competitors. His fame grew, in part, as a result of his paint jobs. Each frame goes through a seven-process paint job which is baked 40 minutes each time. (This is where they derive the name stove enamel finish.) Each frame receives a special rustproofing and primer. Bob Jackson specializes in flamboyant, polychromatic, and enamel paint finishes.

Bob Jackson presently employs four frame builders who receive assistance from two apprentices, and one painter with one painting apprentice. This crew can produce about 25 to 40 frames per week. In 1977, 1,750 Bob Jackson and Merlin frames were built.

Bob Jackson started his own business in 1936, after having worked in the bicycle trade in the north of England. His interest in bicycle frame building resulted from his interest as a bicycle rider. He first started cycling, and racing, in 1929 and subsequently worked for small bicycle builders in Leeds and in Manchester. He learned the most, however, from a frame builder in Manchester called L. H. Brooks. The firm of L. H. Brooks is still in Manchester, but they haven't built bicycle frames since World War II when Mr. Brooks sold his business and emigrated to Canada.

After World War II, Bob Jackson tried to expand his business by opening another shop. He went into partnership with another bicycle enthusiast, Stephen Maurice Woodrup, in 1948. Woodrup and Jackson opened up a store in the Hyde Park section of Leeds, but the partnership was not successful. It was soon dissolved, and by 1952, Woodrup frames were being built by Stephen Maurice Woodrup; Bob Jackson and Merlin frames are being built by JRJ Cycles, Limited.

Building Philosophy

Bob Jackson is a sentimentalist of sorts and this is the reason he builds frames with Merlin decals. As a young man, Bob Jackson rode and raced on Merlin bicycles. Merlin was a custom bicycle builder in London whose reputation can be traced to 1912. When Merlin retired, Bob Jackson didn't want the Merlin name to die away and bought the rights to it.

Bob Jackson is considered an artisan in his trade. When he was asked how long he thought it takes to become a competent frame builder, he (like most frame builders) found the question to be difficult to answer. He feels that it takes years of hard work to become a really skilled builder, especially if the frame builder intends to be able to build to individual specifications. Tubes have to be mitered at the right angles, tube lengths have to be cut precisely, bracket height has to be established accurately, and clearances have to be considered for the type of brakes and wheels being used. Bob Jackson feels that it takes a frame builder years

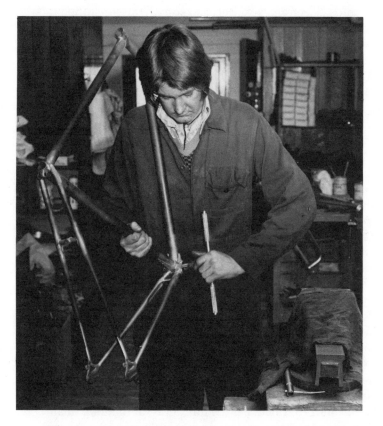

Figure 5-1: "Cleaning" the bottom bracket. Note tool used for this procedure (see figures 3-5 and 3-6 in chapter 3).

before he can alter a specification in midstream without making a "mess of the whole frame."

Bob Jackson no longer builds bicycle frames himself. He is the director of his firm and only makes sure that things are done to his satisfaction. The small detail work and the day-to-day problems encountered in a frame-building shop are handled by John Foster, Bob Jackson's chief frame builder.

John Foster has been building frames for Bob for over 25 years. Originally, John learned how to build frames from a frame builder called Maclean. This was before World War II and Maclean, like so many English builders of the 1920s, went out of business by the late 1950s. Because of John Foster's experience, he is the only one in the firm who builds Reynolds 753 frames.

The Reynolds 753 frames at Bob Jackson are silver-soldered with a rod consisting of 40 percent silver. This same brazing rod is used for the Reynolds 531SL frames that are built there also. Although some builders feel that bronze can be used on the Reynolds 531SL, all agree that there is no alternative with Reynolds 753. Consequently, if you buy a Bob Jackson or Merlin frame, it will be brazed with bronze unless it is of Reynolds 531SL or Reynolds 753. If you do desire one of the Jackson frames made out of 531SL or 753, be prepared to use metric-size components because the tubes that are being used here are all metric.

As far as Reynolds 753 is concerned, currently Raleigh is the only frame manufacturer that has imperial sizes and varied gauges of the tubing available. This is because Gerald O'Donovan at TI Raleigh helped develop the imperial-size tubing.

Bob Jackson and other builders of Reynolds 753 have been limited to metric-size tubing, in only one gauge. However, this may soon change as TI Reynolds continues to expand their line of sizes available. Presently, if you do buy a Reynolds 753 Bob Jackson, they recommend that you use it for light touring (without packs) or for time trialing. The available gauge of tubing is certainly too light for riding on Belgian cobbles or through the mountains with heavy touring packs.

At Bob Jackson, all frames are built entirely without the help of jigs. They do use jigs for the construction of forks, as is common practice. The frames are tacked before they are brazed and they are worked on, from start to finish, by one builder with the help of an apprentice.

Frame Selection

You can get a frame from Bob Jackson with many different options. They now use what is called the oversize Reynolds *Continental fork section* which has only been available to them from Reynolds in the last few years (on Reynolds 531SL and Reynolds 753 only). They do have cast lugs available, but they try not to use them anymore. Bob Jackson claims that the wall thicknesses are never equal on the cast lugs which creates problems when brazing since they must apply more heat at the thicker part of the lug in contrast to less heat on the thinner part.

Figure 5-2: Builder brazing the fork crown at JRJ Cycles.

All in all, Bob Jackson finds the quality of the pressed steel lug far superior to the cast lug.

Don't expect your Bob Jackson to have thinly filed lugs as Bob feels that when the lugs are filed down too thin "they're simply taking away the whole strength of the frame." For him, a lug must only be filed until it is uniformly thick and clean all over.

You can order your Bob Jackson with a cast bottom bracket, but here again Bob prefers not to use cast bottom brackets because he thinks they are poorly finished. He would prefer to use the pressed steel bottom bracket which he feels is clean and uniform in wall thickness.

Fork crowns on Bob Jackson frames are predominantly forged. You can order either a semi-sloping, fully sloping, or flat crown. Bob Jackson doesn't think that the style of the fork crown makes any difference as far as the handling of the bicycle is concerned. He believes the reasons for the varying designs are primarily decorative. He does think that there is a difference in strength, especially with the "Cinelli-type" fork crowns which he says are exceptionally strong. In many cases, he feels that it might be too strong in front impact crashs which can pretzel the fork blades and frame tubes without damaging the crown at all.

Seatstay diameters can be ordered to suit. In Bob's opinion, the ⅝-inch diameter stays are a result of fashion only. He feels that they are just as strong as the ⁹/₁₆ inch or the ½ inch, provided the gauge is the same. He doesn't think that there's a great deal of stress on the seatstays, so that the diameter of the stay is not going to make any difference.

Different seat cluster arrangements are available with a Bob Jackson frame. The full wrap, semi-wrap (chamfered), and the fastback arrangements are all available except on the Reynolds 753, on which you'd get either chamfered or capped clusters. This is because of the heat problem encountered when working with such light tubing. Bob thinks that the wrapover stay is the strongest when using regular Reynolds 531DB.

If you decide you want a Bob Jackson frame, JRJ Cycles, Limited, will build to your specifications. They are willing to build just about anything you want. Bob Jackson cautions the American consumer in particular not to order oversize frames. He is continually amazed as he receives orders from 5'6" customers who order a 24-inch frame.

For reasons we are unable to explain, Bob Jackson frames are somewhat controversial. We interviewed many people who felt that his frames suffered from several undefined (and sometimes mysterious) maladies. This is particularly interesting since virtually everyone rated the overall finish of the framesets as first class. Moreover, our interview with Mr. Jackson revealed that he is extremely conscientious, organized, and knowledgeable.

CHAPTER 6

Mercian Cycles, Limited

Mercian Cycles, Limited
Pontefract Street
Ascot Drive
Derby DE28JD
England

The name Mercian is usually associated with the people who lived in the ancient kingdom of Mercia. The capital of Mercia was located just outside of modern-day Derby where Mercian Cycles is now situated. The showroom and bicycle store is located at 28 Stenson Road while the offices and the frame-building shop are on Pontefract Street. Because of their desire to preserve history, Barker and Crowther decided to call their firm Mercian cycles.

Mercian Cycles started out as a bicycle shop in 1946. Shortly afterward, Barker and Crowther decided to build frames. Almost overnight, their frames and bicycle shop became popular. The demand for their product was almost limitless, but, like other British frame builders, the postwar boom in bicycle frames provided a false confidence in the future demand for their product. The bicycle boom lasted only until 1951, after which a steep decline in sales almost eliminated an entire industry of small frame builders. By the mid-1960s, bicycle sales still looked bleak.

Disenchanted with the pace of the business, Barker and Crowther sold their bicycle/frame-building shop in 1965 to one of their employees, William Betton. Betton had been brought up through the ranks from an apprentice to a full-fledged frame builder and he was anxious to assume the total responsibility for the business. At the age of 25, Betton was not only a frame builder but a bicycle racer as well. He loved to race in all sorts of time trials, from 10 miles to 12 hours, and he still holds the South Pennine Road Club 12-hour record of 247 miles. His enthusiasm for racing paid off in sales of Mercian frames, and Mercian Cycles became the center of bicycling activity in Derbyshire.

Today, Mercian Cycles employs four full-time builders, two assistants, and three painters. Mr. Betton still possesses "the touch" for building frames, but he finds that he has little time to devote to building. Instead, his time is spent on the many other matters related to owning and operating the business.

Background

Most of the builders at Mercian have been brought up through the ranks from apprentice. The only exception is Peter Riches, the chief builder. Peter had several years of experience with various London frame builders before he started working for Mercian in 1952. He is currently involved in designing tandems for Mercian and has designed and built all the jigs for their tandem production. Although Mercian displayed a prototype tandem at the 1977 Harrogate Bicycle Show, they did not go into production until mid-1978. All the tandems are bronze-welded since no lugs are commercially available for the oversize tubing that Peter feels is necessary to insure strength and rigidity.

Two of the builders, Derek Land and Cyril Wagstaff, have been building frames for Mercian for over eight years. Derek is presently in charge of all repairs and Cyril is in charge of quality control and the supervision of the two apprentices. William Betton's close supervision of all operations apparently has paid off. When we asked each English frame builder to rank the top English frame builders, the name Mercian would consistently appear at the top of their lists.

Mercian Cycles is one of the few places where bicycle frames are built on the open hearth rather than by hand-held torches. At Mercian, the builders use a combination of air and natural gas in these open hearths. They believe the advantage of using this method is the decreased possibility of overheating the tubing, unlike a welding torch which can be a "lethal instrument" in the wrong hands. Welding torches are only used at Mercian for repairs or to attach brake cable stops. When using the open hearth technique (as well as any other heating technique), flux is used to help the brazing material flow more easily inside the lug. Cyril Wagstaff points out that, although flux is very helpful in getting the braze to flow, it can also be harmful if too much is used. Cyril recommends using a minimum amount of flux with Reynolds

531SL tubing since it can "eat away at the tube."

In building a frame on the open hearth, Mercian builders use pins to maintain the frame alignment. With the exception of the seatstays and *down tube,* all the tubes are pinned prior to insertion into the hearth. This is something that frame builders who use welding torches seldom do, since heat is localized in one area and an experienced builder is able to hold the joint that he is brazing together by hand, spot-brazing, or by means of a jig.

Building Philosophy

Before a frame is pinned, the builders at Mercian set it up on a primitive jig. They call this step "building the frame on the board." The board is crudely, but functionally, constructed so that its adjustable fittings will accommodate most frame sizes with built-in variables such as *top tube* length, angles, and bottom bracket height.

Mercian Cycles, like most quality frame-building shops, strives to build well-aligned frames. In most cases, this requires considerable knowledge of how the metals will react at varying temperatures. If a problem does occur, the frame builders at Mercian believe that there are fairly wide tolerances with Reynolds 531DB. There are specific tolerances for either *hot setting* or *cold setting.* "Setting" the frame requires a wealth of experience because the margin for error increases as the weight of the tubing decreases. For instance, Reynolds 531SL tubing has less margin for error than regular Reynolds 531DB. With Reynolds 753, a builder does not have any margin for error. Once it is brazed, the frame cannot be bent or twisted to correct for brazing errors. It's got to be built properly from the start.

All Mercian frames are built with *Sifbronze,* the most common braze used in England. The majority of the builders at Mercian prefer the Sifbronze to silver solder since they find that the bronze flows nicely and works particularly well in the open hearth. They find that silver solder is better suited to the welding torch. Most of the builders don't like silver solder because they feel it is softer than the bronze and more prone to cracking when heated. Derek Land has worked with both silver and Sifbronze, and prefers the bronze—"I don't think that there's anything better."

The Mercian top-line frames are built with either regular Reynolds 531DB or with Reynolds 531SL. Although they have discussed offering frames built with Reynolds 753, they have no firm plans. The builders at Mercian see more disadvantages with 753 than advantages. First of all, the tubing is far more expensive and it requires the use of silver solder. This means that they would have to vary their building techniques for Reynolds 753. Although they see it as fantastic tubing, they are presently not willing to risk their good reputation on a tube that obviously is so thin that it can be weakened by very small construction errors. Besides, Mercian has more frame orders than they can handle. The philosophy at Mercian is to only build quality merchandise with tested materials and designs. Mercian is sometimes more cautious than other frame builders, but they believe that they owe their customers reliable products backed by their many years of experience.

Production at this small Derby frame shop is 25 to 30 frames per week. Each frame is built from start to finish by the same builder with help from an apprentice. After the frame and fork have been completely brazed, they are allowed to cool. Next, the small holes that have been drilled to release the heat are filled with small pieces of steel. Mercian believes this step is important because it keeps the water out when riding and if the frame and fork go to be *chrome plated* it will keep acid out of these parts also.

The painting is done at the rear of the frame shop where spray booths and *baking ovens* are set up. They would not reveal their secret methods of stove enamelling since they believe they have developed an unmatched combination of beauty and resistance to chipping. At Mercian, they pride themselves on their paint job. They are very accommodating in requests for custom colors, and they will try to match any color a customer provides. If you have a specific color in mind for your frame, send them a sample of the color. They will try to match it. One word of advice from Mercian Cycles on paint: If you want a really smooth and even finish, order an enamel paint. Be cautious when ordering silver or flamboyant finishes, since they tend to accentuate any imperfections in the finish of the lug or tubing in spite of extensive preparation of the frame before application of the finish color.

After brazing, each frame is sandblasted. All the frames then receive a base undercoat that is air-dried. If a frame is going to be painted white, it is given a quick white undercoat before giving it the white topcoat. The frame is then stove-enamelled and in-

63

spected. If it passes their inspection, it is given a coat of special clear varnish. If not, the paint is rubbed out and the frame is repainted.

Putting on the coat of clear varnish is the last, and probably the most difficult, step in the entire process. The clear varnish is very difficult to handle because the painter cannot see it as it is applied. Consequently, the painters spraying the varnish are the most experienced in the shop.

Frame Selection

At Mercian they will build custom frames to your specifications on request. They will design the frame using your vital statistics such as height and leg length, but, like most builders, they would prefer that you send them the specific measurements and use of the frame that you want built.

If you would like them to fit you on a frame, their basic points of measurement are the inside length of your leg and your "reach" (the length of your arms and trunk). The purpose of the bicycle (touring or track racing) will determine the angles of the frame. If you specify frame measurements that are unsafe or unsound, they will advise against them and will provide their recommendations.

Unless otherwise specified, all the frames at Mercian are built with a top tube length that has been based on a mean average resulting from years of experience. Although it is not a foolproof method, they feel that it will suit most individuals with minimal adjustments in the height of the saddle and the length of the stem.

The lugs used at Mercian are stamped steel. They have eight different styles in stock and the top three types are handcut and drilled. They believe that there is a trend toward the fancy lug which was popular with touring cyclists prior to World War II. Although the smooth-lined lug is still enormously popular, they have been receiving more requests for the ornate lugs. All lugs are purchased for a standard 73/73-degree design and then are adjusted if required. Like the vast majority of the famous frame builders, they do not believe that the lugs should be filed too thinly. Although this style has recently gained popularity in the United States, most builders agree with Derek Land when he says: "It seems pointless to put a lug on, which is the thing that holds it all together, and then file it away!"

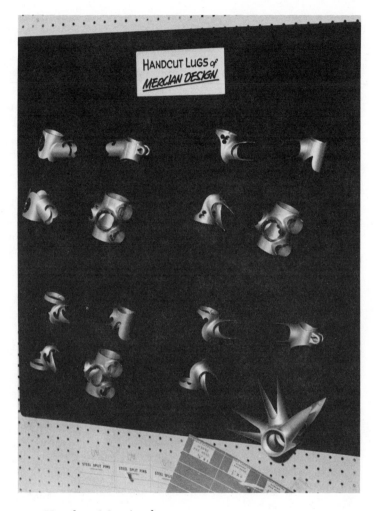

Figure 6-1: Handcut Mercian lugs.

They have tried using cast lugs, but they feel that the cast lug is too heavy. They use cast fork crowns but they are not totally pleased with them because of the added time needed to properly finish a cast product which is usually very rough and pitted. They prefer to use a *flat top* (pressed) crown which comes from the manufacturer "in really good condition."

Three types of seatstay clusters are used on Mercian frames: full wrap, semi-wrap, and fastback. Mercian uses a fastback stay that butts into the seat tube. Although this fastback cluster is not believed to be as strong as the full or semi-wrap, it is sometimes preferred because of its reduced weight. If a fastback cluster is built correctly, there should be little chance of failure. A builder, however, has to be very careful when brazing a fastback stay because the stays are butted onto the seat tube which is the thinnest of the frame tubes and the seat tube is not butted at the top making it very susceptible to overheating.

At Mercian they only use ½-inch and ⅝-inch diameter seatstays. The 9/16-inch stays have been dropped because the demand is presently for the chunkier look of the ⅝-inch stay. The ½-inch stay is standard on 19½ to 20½-inch frame sizes. Consequently, if you need a small frame and want the ⅝-inch stay, you must specifically request it. The ½-inch stay is used on the smaller frames because it gives a more balanced appearance.

Regardless of the quality of the frame, the people at Mercian caution that it will be inefficient if it does not properly fit the rider. Derek Land believes that "You could possibly have Eddy Merckx and if he had the wrong angles and the wrong top tube and possibly the wrong size within a quarter of an inch, it wouldn't be quite as good as another frame that was the right size."

They believe that the rider must experiment to find the right frame, but once he has found the frame that's really right for him, he should stick with it. In other words, once you have found your ideal, there's no point in changing the design unless you want to change the use of the bike (i.e., you have a touring bicycle but you would like a track bike).

To summarize, Mercian offers custom frames that are truly one of a kind. They will build to individual specifications, paint any color requested, and provide fancy cut lugs. It is rare to find a builder with such a strong reputation that will spend the time necessary to build a frame that is truly unique.

CHAPTER 7

Harry Quinn Cycles, Limited

Harry Quinn Cycles, Limited
7/9 Walton Road
Liverpool, Merseyside L4 4PL
England

The firm of Harry Quinn Cycles began frame building during the reign of Queen Victoria. Harry's father started the firm in 1901. Since that time the firm has been producing custom frames. Until the 1940s, the custom frames built by the Quinn family were called Coronets. In 1945, the name was changed to Harry Quinn. Since 1949, each Harry Quinn frame has been numbered consecutively and, as of September 26, 1977, 4,206 frames had been made. In fact, up until 1973, all Harry Quinn frames were made personally by Harry.

Today, Harry shares the frame-building responsibilities with one other frame builder, whom Harry has trained, and two apprentices. While Harry is presently the chief frame builder of Harry Quinn Cycles, he will be retiring in a few years. Plans have been made that will insure that Harry Quinn Cycles will continue operating as one of Liverpool's finest bicycle stores and frame-building shops.

Frank Clements purchased Harry Quinn Cycles in February 1977 and has retained Harry as his chief frame builder and design consultant. Although Harry is the master builder, he has two more important functions at this time. First, he supervises the production of all frames built. Secondly, he is responsible for the training and development of competent frame builders in order to insure the future quality of Harry Quinn frames. Harry believes in continuing the line of master builders.

Frank Clements is certainly not a new name in cycling. In fact, everyone in the bicycle industry in England has heard of the Clements brothers. All of the brothers have been active racers who turned to employment in the bicycle industry after their retirement from competition. Perhaps the most illustrious member of the Clements family is brother Ernie who won a silver medal for Great Britain in the 1948 Olympic road race and is now director of Falcon Cycles.

Background

Frank Clements raced from 1953 to 1961 in Britain and on the Continent. After his racing years, Frank began working with his brother Ernie at Falcon Cycles. Frank felt the need for more independence so he started a bicycle import business, JHF Cycle Distributors, whose offices have been located, since 1975, in the same building that houses Harry Quinn Cycles. Frank's involvement with Harry Quinn started as a result of renting office space from Harry. This involvement led to the purchase of Harry Quinn Cycles on February 14, 1977.

Utilizing his knowledge gained from racing and his experience from working in the cycle trade, Frank Clements has developed a propensity to analyze the critical aspects of frame design and, most importantly, verbalize his views. He is able to offer many tips to the uninformed enthusiast in search of a quality product.

According to Frank, the quality of a frameset is easiest to determine if it is examined immediately after brazing. If a frame has not been sandblasted, you should be able to see the brass around the lug. If there is brass on the tube, the builder has probably been sloppy and the frame tubes have been overheated. Nearly all the British manufacturers that Frank has seen, braze from the outside of the tube. When examining the bottom bracket, you should be able to see the brass around the bottom of the tubes as they intersect in the bottom bracket. Frank claims that a majority of the Italian builders braze from the inside out. The advantage in this method is that, when a builder brazes from the inside of the bottom bracket, he makes sure that there is brass at the end of the tubes that go into the bottom bracket. To check if the tubes have been overheated during assembly, Frank recommends running a file on the tube adjacent to the lug. If the tube has not been overheated, the file will dig into the tube. If the file bounces over the surface, it is an indication that the tube has been overheated and that it is brittle. Once the frame is sandblasted and painted, a lot of building mistakes are hidden. After painting, it is impossible to check for the color of the tubes (another check for overheating) or the resistance of the tube to a file. Although gaps between the lug and the tube are not conclusive evidence of a poorly built frame, they do raise the possibility that there is not brazing all the way through the joint.

Figure 7-1: Harry Quinn with a complete main triangle of a frame. The jig for brazing is on Harry's right.

Frank feels that the best way to test a bicycle is to ride it. If it feels lively and you are able to sit up and ride with no hands in a straight line, you have some indication that the frame has been built correctly. Frank says that he is constantly amazed at the number of custom frames that will not track correctly, although they are alleged to have been built by specialists.

Frank believes that many people are swayed by fashion when choosing a frame, since there are few people capable of explaining the advantages or disadvantages of different designs. For instance, a couple of years ago it was in vogue to have a fork built with a fully sloping Cinelli crown. There is nothing inherently wrong with the crown except that it is usually too stiff for long races on rutted or bumpy roads. According to Frank, many of the bicycle fashions start in Italy, the "home of bicycles, top-quality bicycles. Anything that deals with bicycles can be had in Italy, even the machinery to manufacture bicycles."

Building Philosophy

Harry Quinn has been building frames, using essentially the same methods, for 45 years. His interest in bicycles started as a young boy when he learned the basics of frame building from his father. His interest was further developed while racing prior to World War II (1935–37). His racing experience was strictly as a time trialist, as there was little else being promoted in England. But even this limited racing experience ignited the motivation required for Harry to devote the rest of his working days to frame building. There are few frame builders who had as many years' experience as Harry or who can trace their frame-building history as far back as Harry can. When asked what it takes to become a frame builder, Harry answered, "If you have a young chap who's good with his hands and has a very good method of work, he can be building good frames in 12 months. You can get another chap and it could take three or four years and he's still not able to build a good frame. It's like any other craft. If you haven't got the aptitude and talent, you'll never do it."

Harry believes that the demise of many frame builders has been caused by trying to manufacture more than they are really capable of producing. Many frame builders succumb to the temptation of cutting corners to meet demand. At Harry Quinn

Cycles, they have resisted the pressure to meet demand and instead have striven to maintain the quality that brought them fame. At Harry Quinn, they spend a lot of time just cleaning up the lug, for instance. According to Harry, "You needn't do it, but it's a sign of workmanship."

In order to insure consistent quality and workmanship in his frames, Harry will not build more than one per day. He believes that a frame must be carefully mitered and brazed. Most important is the need to keep the frame in proper alignment while brazing. It is not acceptable to build a frame out of track and then bend it back into track. A frame can be twisted back in line after it has been built, but it will eventually come out of track after hard use.

Harry uses the Sifbronze on all his Reynolds 531DB frames. He uses silver on regular Reynolds 531DB frames when brazing on fittings. On the Reynolds 531SL and on the Reynolds 753, Harry uses silver solder. Reynolds has just authorized Harry as a Reynolds 753 builder and Frank has ordered 95 sets in anticipation of the demand. Frank believes that Reynolds 753 is an incredible material that has yet to reach its full popularity. "We have put a 753 fork in the vise and hit it with a hammer and there's just no way that you'll bend it. The tubing is that strong."

Harry finds that working with silver solder is not much different than working with Sifbronze. The biggest difference is the melting temperature. The only problem encountered with silver is when a frame builder overheats the frame and gets oxidation. At that point the silver will not penetrate the lug.

Harry prefers to use Prugnat pressed lugs and he will cut by hand on request. Harry has used cast lugs in the past but finds the quality of cast lugs to be very poor and the angle cannot be changed to suit the individual requirements of a custom order. There is no flexibility in design; the frame design has to suit the cast lugs that are available.

The Italian section fork blades are now available on Reynolds 753 and Reynolds 531SL. Reynolds does not provide Harry with the larger fork sections on regular Reynolds 531DB. Most fork crowns that Harry uses are Cinelli semi-sloping cast crowns. He does use pressed fork crowns, but generally prefers the quality of the cast crowns. He offers many different types of seatstay cluster arrangements and finds very little difference in strength and performance among them.

All the frames are designed on what Harry calls his "Ouija board." The adjustable sections on the board were built by Harry and adjust to given parameters for various frame sizes. For example, if a customer wants a 23-inch frame with 73-degree parallel angles, the board can be adjusted for these dimensions. The wheelbase and top tube length become immediately obvious. Every frame is fitted to the board throughout the frame-building process to insure accurate construction. All the tubes are mitered before they are brazed to the lug. According to Harry, a perfect miter is essential for a strong frame. The frames are brazed together without the help of pins. Harry believes that the use of pins is only needed on mass-production frames and on the hearth-brazed frames.

Figure 7-2: Harry's "Ouija board" for frame setup. The clipboards on the left contain specific frame geometry requested by the customer.

Frame Selection

Standard top tube lengths are calculated by subtracting ½ inch from the frame size but, as with most frame builders, this does not apply to the small or to the large frame sizes. Building for the large or small frame sizes requires different techniques. For a 25-inch frame, Harry will build it with a 24-inch top tube but this requires dropping the seat tube from the regular 73 degrees to about 72 degrees. Then he lifts the head tube to about 74 degrees to get the wheels in the right position. Otherwise the front wheel will be "28 inches in front of the rider" and the rear wheel "miles out." The 74-degree *head angle* will bring the front wheel further underneath the bicycle which will permit a decent fork rake, thus giving it good "steerability." With a small frame, it's just the opposite. Harry builds them with a steeper seat angle and a shallower head angle.

When sizing a customer for a bicycle frame, Harry likes to see what the customer's full height is compared to the inside leg measurement. He likes to be able to know if he has a tall person with short legs or a tall person with long legs. This helps him decide size as well as top tube length. A basic rule of thumb for determining frame size at Harry Quinn is to subtract 9 inches from the inseam measurement. Variations on this occur because Harry believes that a racing frame should be ½ inch smaller. This gives the rider the option of lifting the saddle a bit more while keeping the handlebars low, thus giving the racer a more aerodynamic position.

When Harry builds a frame for touring, he usually builds it with a slightly longer wheelbase than he would if it were a racing bicycle. Specifically, he lengthens the chainstays. This he does primarily to accommodate larger gear clusters in the rear. If a tourist is going to use only close ratios, there is no problem with the short chainstays but the larger freewheels do require 16¾-inch chainstays. With the smooth road surfaces that are found in the United States and in the United Kingdom, Harry sees no reason why a tourist shouldn't use "more of a racing design for touring." Harry does, however, caution that even with improved road surfaces a longer wheelbase bicycle with a lower bottom bracket will perform better on long touring rides. The need for a longer wheelbase becomes more important when the bicycle is loaded down with gear.

For 40 years, Harry Quinn has been the bicycle mentor of the Liverpool cycling community. Many riders still come to see Harry to discuss their individual bicycle problems. Harry is easy to talk to and is able to solve problems analytically. He is different from some builders who won't change simply because that's the way they have always done it. Harry is objective in his decisions.

If you are interested in a Harry Quinn frame, it can only be purchased through Harry's bicycle store which occupies the first floor of the Walton Road address. (The frame shop occupies the second floor.) By writing to Harry Quinn, you can receive his order blank, and Harry will custom-build a frame to suit your specifications.

Harry Quinn is one of the last of the famous builders who has refused to succumb to the temptations of gaining increased profit through increased production. His frames tend to be quite conservative in both design and finish. Harry believes that a frame should be strong and well finished—not flashy.

CHAPTER 8

Jack Taylor Cycles

Jack Taylor Cycles
Church Road
Stockton on Tees
Cleveland County TS 18 2LY
England

Jack Taylor Cycles is owned and operated by the three Taylor brothers—Jack, Norman, and Ken. Jack Taylor Cycles is unique in that its tandem production is almost equal to its single frame production. In addition to tandems, the Taylors build other specialty cycles such as triplets and tricycles. Eighty percent of these specialty products are exported, the majority of which find their way to customers in the United States. Today the Taylors have a thriving business. Their success story is not one of circumstances or luck. It is the result of many years of determination and hard work.

The Taylors' interest in bicycles stems from when Jack was a teenager in the 1930s. The first bicycle that Jack owned was a Raleigh Sports model. His grandfather purchased the bicycle at a cost of $20. With two fixed sprockets and Lucas chrome bell, the bike was an improvement over the "dreadnoughts" of the 1920s and 1930s, but a far cry from today's lightweight bicycle.

Jack loved his bicycle and rode it everywhere. The more he rode, the more riders he met who shared his cycling interests. In his travels, he discovered a hard-core riding group that had "fancy" lightweight bicycles—Merlins and Claud Butlers. As soon as Jack laid his eyes on these lightweight beauties, a new level of interest was opened. In those days, there was a scarcity of good bicycles. Jack soon found that he could not afford a lightweight bicycle that would meet his quality requirements.

Background

Jack's next step was a logical one. Since he could not afford a bicycle of his choice, he would design and build his own. Although he was an idealist, Jack had the ability to objectively evaluate his ideas. He dreamed of riding the Tour de France with Coppi and Bartali, his heroes. Yet he knew that he didn't possess the ingredients necessary to become a world champion cyclist. Instead of concentrating on the development of his cycling skills, he spent his waking hours refining his skills in designing and building bicycle frames.

Jack started building bicycles in 1936. Because of his enthusiasm and technical skills, he was able to persuade two of his riding friends to go into business with him. For Jack, going into business was a simple process. He and two friends, Lance Bell and Jack Hood, set up a shop in a little green shed in the back of his mother's house on Greta Road in Stockton. During this time, the operation in the green shed was more of a hobby since all three men were employed elsewhere.

Jack Taylor, of course, was the most active member of the threesome. It had been Jack's idea to use the green shed as a frame workshop because it was only a few feet from his house. Fortunately, Jack's enthusiasm was not as limited as his finances. His only source of light in the shed was a single light bulb connected to the wiring circuit in the house. This way, he was able to work at night when he came home from work. Since watches and clocks were luxuries that Jack could not afford, he connected a makeshift loudspeaker to the house radio and ran the wire from the house to the shed. He would become so engrossed in what he was doing that he would forget the time and end up going to bed far past midnight. Since Jack had to be up very early in the morning, he found that his ingenious loudspeaker worked well. Now he could hear the eight o'clock news, the nine o'clock news, and the ten o'clock news. When Jack heard the ten o'clock news he would quit for the evening.

Jack's green shed became the center of bicycling activity in Stockton. He was constantly surrounded by the "elitist" cycling element. With all the activity that was going on in that green shed, it was difficult not to interest Jack's younger brothers, Norman and Ken. Soon Ken and Norman, who were as mechanically inclined as Jack, started helping out their older brother with increasing enthusiasm.

The original threesome of Lance Bell, Jack Hood, and Jack Taylor did not last very long. Jack Hood and Lance Bell loved bicycling, but they just didn't have the devotion to technical details that Jack Taylor did. As a result, the partnership was dissolved and Jack Taylor Cycles became a family operation. Once Jack started to build his own bicycles and found that he could sell them, he began a systematic plan of building a bicycle factory. Officially, Jack Taylor Cycles became a business in 1945, when Jack and his brothers opened a bank account and each of the brothers put in 20 pounds. Typical of Jack's kindhearted personality, he ended up putting in 40 pounds since one of his brothers did not have the money. In 1946, Jack Taylor Cycles had its first official balance sheet.

Figure 8-1: Jack (left) and Norman Taylor inspect a newly brazed tandem frame.

Building Philosophy

It must be remembered that Jack Taylor started building bicycles in his green shed as a hobby. Bicycles were very expensive compared to the wages of the day, and as a result, Jack started building bicycles because he allegedly couldn't afford to buy one. This is only partially true. Jack had invested his money in a Claud Butler tandem and a Butler racing frame. A lot of Jack's inspiration came from owning the Claud Butlers. In later years when Jack finally met Claud Butler at a London Bicycle Show, Claud asked Jack what had made him start building bicycles. Without being solicitious Jack told him: "It was partly from buying one of yours. We were that keen on the way they were

Figure 8-2: Jack Taylor fits the bottom bracket on a custom tandem.

made. We got so much pleasure out of them that it fired our imaginations and we wanted to do it.''

What started out as a hobby in 1936 became the beginning of a lifetime occupation in 1942, when Jack Taylor bought a parcel of land in the center of Stockton from the Stockton Corporation. Jack had plans of a giant complex which would mass-produce bicycles in Stockton. His bubble burst in 1951 when bicycle sales started to

Figure 8-3: Norman Taylor in his workshop with the simple Taylor-design fork jig.

rapidly decline. "It didn't matter what we did, how much money we spent, we just couldn't sell bicycles to people who wanted to sit in a motorcar."

In 1939 England declared war on Germany, but the Taylor brothers were fortunate in that they never did see the front lines. They remained in Stockton for the duration and were assigned to war work. During the war, there wasn't a good bicycle to be found at any price. As a result, the production of the garden shed was now really in demand. The Taylors were, however, running into supply problems. They couldn't buy lugs, for instance. Jack had previously taken some night classes in bronze welding and decided to try to build the bicycles without lugs. The bronze welding worked so well that today most of the Taylor's bicycles are still bronze-welded.

Although the Taylors were seriously involved with bicycle building, they still found time to train and race with the Stockton Wheelers. The Taylors' first introduction to racing came in time trials; however, this event did not interest them because it was a "cloak and dagger sport." The races were always run at six o'clock on a Sunday morning when the least amount of traffic was anticipated on the road. Dressed all in black, each rider would leave at one-minute intervals.

The Taylors found this to be very boring and when Percy Stallard of Wolverhampton formed a rebel movement of bicycle riders in 1942, the Taylors were among the first to join. This rebel movement was quickly suspended from the National Cyclists' Union, the controlling body of racing cyclists in the United Kingdom.

Percy Stallard's group then formed the British League of Racing Cyclists. They held regular road races using road bicycles as opposed to the fixed gears used by the time trialists. The BLRC was exactly to the Taylors' liking. Jack openly admits that he was a horrible time trialist but found that he was decent as a road racer: "I was not much good at time trials when I went with all the crack riders. In fact, we weren't much good at anything. We were just very enthusiastic. Of course, when you got into the first half dozen in a race with the top guys from all over the country you thought, 'By golly, I'm better than I thought I was.' "

The road racing circuit that the BLRC developed filled a vacuum in Jack's riding career. Jack and his brothers could actually ride races "continental style," as a team. Jack says, "We called ourselves 'independents'. We broke all the rules of the amateur classes, our jerseys had Jack Taylor Cycles on them."

Probably the most important race ridden by the Jack Taylor Cycles team was the Brighton to Glasgow, the forerunner of the Milk Race, England's most prestigious road race. The Taylor brothers rode this race as a team five times from 1945 to 1949. The Taylors loved "getting all dressed up" in their special embroidered jerseys that they had ordered from Belgium. Each team member had two jerseys to insure having a fresh one every morning during stage races.

After the 1945 Brighton to Glasgow race, Ken lost his job as a result of being absent five days. Since the Taylors had already partially constructed their "bicycle factory" on the land they had purchased from the Stockton Corporation, Ken went to work full time at Jack Taylor Cycles. Business was good and a year later Norman, and then Jack, joined Ken.

Development of the works progressed quickly in both the expansion of the facilities and in the production of bicycles. At one time, there were nine employees. Once the bicycle boom after World War II ended, so did the rapid growth of Jack Taylor Cycles. The large factory that Jack had once envisioned never materialized, but something else did—a friendly custom frame shop with a six- to eighteen-month waiting list for its specialized products.

The Taylors are the nicest, friendliest people you'd ever hope to meet. After 40 years, they are still enthusiastic riders. Norman rides centuries with his friends every weekend during the season. He jokingly claims he gets 100 miles to the gallon because on the 100-mile rides they invariably stop and visit some of the country pubs along the way. Jack still rides the same bike he rode in the 1949 Brighton to Glasgow race! He also rides it to work.

The Taylors believe that a good frame builder has to have a lot of enthusiasm for his product. Jack explains it best: "We know what we're making the bicycle for and to us it's the most beautiful thing imaginable, a new bicycle. Bicycles have some magic about them to us. You put a bit of yourself into these bicycles, like an artist does with his paintings. Ours are all one-of-a-kind specials for some particular person. I don't say everything you do comes out perfect, but the ideal is that you're aiming for perfection."

Frame Selection

Around 1956, a young couple from Stockton, California, decided to come to Stockton, England, to buy a Jack Taylor tandem. It was the first Taylor tandem purchased by Americans. This couple was the first of many Americans to walk through the doors of the Taylor works on Church Road; now most of the 200 bicycles that are made by the Taylors each year come to the United States. Since the Taylors do not advertise, their sales are generated strictly by word of mouth. The Taylors explain their success with Americans by one simple statement: "Our tandems are built in the way that Americans want to buy them."

The tandems are all built with Reynolds 531 plain gauge tubing. The Taylors have used Reynolds 531DB but found that the frame had too much flex. To insure a more stable ride, all the tandems are built with specially ordered oversize Reynolds tubes. The down tube is the heaviest tube at 18 gauge. The oval bottom tube is 19 gauge, as are the chainstays. The Taylors readily admit that their tandem frames are heavy, but they believe that the tandems have to be in order to be rigid enough for two people to ride.

As a result of the special tubes used on the tandem, there are no lugs made to fit. Consequently, all the tandems are bronze-welded without lugs. This also gives the builder more flexibility in custom-fitting sizes. By not using lugs, a builder does not have to be concerned with stocking a large number of lugs for each different frame angle.

Although most of the Taylor frames are lugless, they do make a number with lugs. These appear only on "single" frames. The lugs and bottom brackets are pressed steel. A cast bottom bracket is available upon request. Norman likes to use the cast bottom bracket because he feels the threads are generally better and it makes the frame more rigid. Norman also likes semi-sloping cast fork crowns. He finds them easy to work with.

Any kind of seat cluster arrangement can be ordered but Norman does not recommend the Italian fastback for touring because of clearance problems. Sifbronze is used for brazing, with occasional use of silver for brazed-on fittings. All the frames are tacked and those with lugs are built freehand, while those without lugs (including tandems) are built on jigs.

Something very interesting about Taylor frames is a constant design feature—the Taylors like to keep the head angle at 73 degrees. They believe this is necessary for good steering. If changes in top tube length are necessary, the Taylors feel it's preferable to make them by varying the angle of the seat tube. The angles on racing and touring bicycles they build are generally similar. The biggest difference is the longer wheelbase for a touring bicycle created by the use of longer chainstays and a larger fork rake.

If you are thinking of buying a Jack Taylor frame or complete bicycle, it is best to send them the exact size that you want. The Taylors make no pretense about being expert fitters. They feel a person should know what size bicycle he or she wants. They consider themselves expert frame builders, not fitters.

If you would like to order just a frame, be sure to tell the Taylors exactly what components you plan on using. This is most important when ordering a tandem frame since their tandem tubing is larger than standard tubing. You must tell them what kind of brakes, derailleurs, and other components, because of the many fittings needed to make a tandem frame functional.

Although the Taylors make racing frames, their specialty is touring and tandem frames. Norman makes all the touring racks as well as all the braze-on fittings used to attach racks, fenders, and lights. When requested, Norman also builds touring frames with special pannier supports.

All the sandblasting and painting is done on the premises. The Taylors even make all their own shipping crates. Their little operation is quite efficient with the work being delegated among the threesome. Norman builds all the frames, Jack does the painting, and Ken installs the components and sends the frames and bicycles out. Once the frame or bicycle is completed and packed, it is airfreighted from Stockton and can be delivered anyplace in the world within 48 hours. As a special touch (the Taylor way of saying thank you), each Taylor customer finds an attractive Taylor feeder bag packed with their brand-new Jack Taylor.

In summary, the Taylors are extremely anxious to please every customer. They will custom-build a frameset to your requested specifications. Most important for the often-neglected tourist, they specialize in touring frames that are designed to accommodate your personal choice of panniers. Jack Taylor Cycles was unique among the many builders we visited. They are committed to meeting the needs of the recreational cyclist.

CHAPTER 9

TI Raleigh, Limited

TI Raleigh, Limited
177 Lenton Boulevard
Nottingham NG7 27B
England

TI Raleigh is located in the central region of England, appropriately called the Midlands. It was here that the industrial revolution found its beginnings and witnessed many of the innovations and inventions that gave rise to large-scale manufacturing.

The largest portion of the TI Raleigh complex is located in Nottingham. There are also factories in Ilkeston and in Worksop which produce bicycles, and two factories in Birmingham which produce bicycle parts. From its humble beginnings in Nottingham in 1886, where production was about three bicycles per week, TI Raleigh has grown into the largest producer of quality bicycles in the world, manufacturing over two million bicycles per year.

The history of the Raleigh bicycle begins, most appropriately, in a small workshop on Raleigh Street in Nottingham, England. Three workmen, Woodhead, Angois, and Ellis, began building bicycles in 1886. Since their bicycles were well designed and well constructed, they had no trouble selling them. Their popularity came to the attention of an enthusiastic cyclist, Frank Bowden, who had been looking for more than a new bicycle for himself.

Frank Bowden was a successful lawyer who had just returned to England from the Far East, ill but with a small fortune. Financially secure, Bowden turned his attention to a search for medical cures for his illness:

> I arrived in England troubled by an inactive liver, sleeplessness, bad circulation, varicose veins, rheumatism and general debility. The result was a very weak condition of body and but little energy of mind (Bowden 1975, p. 13).

Background

Frank Bowden went from doctor to doctor without finding a cure. Finally, he met a physician at the Harrogate spa who advised him to take up cycling. His cure was almost miraculous. Within four months, his health was restored and he began to think very seriously about introducing people to the benefits of cycling. He was so enthusiastic about the sport that in December 1888 he negotiated the purchase of the little workshop on Raleigh Street and thus founded the Raleigh Bicycle Company. Raleigh continued to grow through two world wars and the many ups and downs of the bicycle market. From those early beginnings, the Raleigh Bicycle Company has expanded to the point that the factory in Nottingham alone employs 8,500 people in a complex that covers 64 acres.

Another British bicycle company in Birmingham, Tube Investments, better known as TI, shared Raleigh's spectacular growth. Both TI and Raleigh had grown by good management and the acquisition of other bicycle companies. By 1959, both companies dominated sales throughout much of the world. In 1960 they decided to quit competing with each other and merged into the company known today as TI Raleigh. After the merger, it was decided that the bicycle production would be handled in Nottingham and the component manufacturing would be handled in Birmingham.

The three TI Raleigh bicycle factories in the United Kingdom (Nottingham, Worksop, Ilkeston) are all located within a 40-mile radius and each has its own specialty. The Nottingham factory produces what Raleigh terms the "bread and butter" bicycles. These include children's, adult tourist, small-wheel, and adult sports bicycles. All of these bicycles are 1-, 3-, or 5-speed models. A few 10-speeds are made in Nottingham, but these are generally the lower-priced models.

In the late 1950s, Raleigh felt that it was imperative to have a section devoted to the production of quality hand-built bicycles and by 1960, they concluded negotiations for the purchase of the famous Carlton factory located near the edge of Sherwood Forest in Worksop, England.

Today, the Carlton factory produces about eighty-two thousand bicycles per year, bearing either the Raleigh or Carlton names. All Raleigh bicycles that are built with Reynolds 531 are

85

made at the Carlton factory in Worksop.

The original Carlton factory was located in Carlton, England, not far from Worksop. The first Carlton bicycles were made by the village smithy, Fred Hanstock, in 1896. As a result of the popularity of the bicycles, the factory was moved to the larger facilities in Worksop in the 1930s. Daniel R. O'Donovan was employed as general manager in 1937 and he became so enamored with his work that in 1939 he bought the business. His sons, Gerald and Kevin, shared their father's interest, and as schoolboys they spent all their free time at their father's factory. Gerald, who was studying structural engineering, found the Carlton factory to be an endless challenge as he explored the technical aspect of bicycle manufacturing. Eventually, he was allowed to help in the frame-building operations and review the engineering designs for the different Carlton models. His frame-building career officially started in 1937 and he is still actively building and designing frames. Kevin's interest was centered around the marketing aspect of the business which led to his current position as the managing director of TI Raleigh's South African operation.

At the Worksop factory, only the track bicycles and the custom bicycles are individually brazed on an open hearth. All the other bicycles are ring-brazed on a specially designed machine. A Raleigh bicycle frame goes through a myriad of operations on the highly mechanized production line at the Worksop factory.

Building Philosophy

All the frames built on the production line have mitered tubes except for the tube ends that go into the bottom bracket. The tubes are mitered and fitted into the lugs with a ring of brass inserted between the tube and the lug. When the joint is heated, the brass flows throughout the lug and solidly binds the joint. Next, the tubes are drilled for ventilation and the lugs are hand-filed to insure uniformity. The tubes for the regular production bicycles are not pinned before the brazing operation; they are coppered (a quick tack-brazing operation using copper instead of brass) to insure proper alignment. Copper is used because it melts at a higher temperature than brass. When the frame is ring-brazed with brass, the tubes will stay in place since the brass will flow before the copper reaches its melting point.

With the ring-brazing method, the frame joints are first

copper-tacked with hand-held torches. Once the entire frame is completely copper-tacked, it is placed on the ring-brazing machine. The machine then brazes all the tubes that go into the bottom bracket, the head lug and its tubes, and finally the seat lug. The machine holds the entire frame while each joint is blasted in turn with gas jets at a set time and temperature. After each joint is completely brazed, the machine rotates the frame (like a windmill) into position to braze the next joint. This process continues until the whole bicycle frame is brazed. The top-line frames are ring-brazed on these machines, but the timing and temperature are set differently for Reynolds 531DB frames. The machine applies the heat more slowly and at a slightly lower temperature. The brazing on the machine is done with a combination of acetylene and oxygen. Unlike the frames, the forks are built by hand. The fork blades are pinned to the fork crowns and they are brazed with hand-held torches.

Once the bicycle frame and the fork are brazed, they are sent to the refinement department. Here, frames and forks are cleaned of any excess brass with hand-held torches using natural gas before they undergo the second filing operation. Everything is filed by air-driven belt files before the frame and fork are faced, bored, and threaded by machine. Every frame and fork is then checked for trueness. Each frame and fork go through the sulfuric acid pickling tanks twice, before and after the final filing. Putting the frame and fork through the pickling tanks serves to clean them and to prepare the metal for the paint. TI Raleigh had sandblasted the frames until they found that the pickling process caused less damage and increased the ability of the paint to adhere to the metal.

After each dip in the pickling tank, the frame and fork are oven-dried. Frames and forks are then primed and painted by hand in individual painting booths. Each frame and fork receives three or four coats of paint including the undercoating. If a frame or fork requires chroming, it is sent to the Raleigh complex in Nottingham.

All of the remaining assembly operations needed to complete the bicycle are performed by hand. Although the Carlton factory tried automatic wheel-building machines, they were unable to equal the previous productivity of the department because of excessive downtime. Consequently, they decided it was more productive to hand-build wheels.

Eddie Haslehurst, the foreman of the Carlton factory frame

shop and an employee of Carlton since 1930, shows pride in his workmanship as do many of his co-workers. Many of Eddie's co-workers have been employed at Carlton all their working lives—the Carlton factory is their second home. Their attitude is best reflected in Eddie's own words: "We like it here at Carlton and we try to make sure that the work done here is special."

In 1974, TI Raleigh completed its Ilkeston factory. The factory was constructed to respond to the demands of TI Raleigh's increased involvement in racing. TI Raleigh knew that they would need to further develop their racing bicycle if their growing status among racers was to continue. The Carlton factory was originally purchased for this purpose in 1960, but a growing bicycle market changed the production of the Carlton factory from 2,500 bicycles per year to almost 30 times that per year. Consequently, the Carlton factory was no longer suitable for the individual one-of-a-kind production needed for top professionals.

The specialty bicycle section was moved in 1974 from Worksop to a new factory in Ilkeston, Derbyshire. Because of his technical skills, Gerald O'Donovan was put in charge of the new specialty factory. The building is quite small in comparison to the rest of the TI Raleigh operation—it only encompasses about 12,000 square feet of floor space. Fortunately, the intent of the facility has remained unchanged—the volume of bicycles produced is secondary to the innovation and quality of the product. The Ilkeston factory is best described as a test laboratory rather than a factory, and its emphasis on research has resulted in several major cycling breakthroughs.

In the 1960s Gerald O'Donovan devoted much of his energy to finding lighter tubing for bicycle production. He looked first at *carbon fiber* and he produced a prototype carbon fiber frame that was first shown at the Anaheim Aerospace Materials Convention in 1968. The primary problem with the carbon fiber frame was the lack of an acceptable method of fastening the tubes; they had to be glued. Although carbon fiber is stiffer than steel, it is unsuitable for bicycle frames because of the lack of strength of the joints which are epoxied together. Since the weakest link in a frame is its joint, the carbon frames were unable to equal the stiffness of a "normal" Reynolds 531DB frame because no one has discovered a glue that is as stiff as carbon fiber itself. O'Donovan's dissatisfaction with his carbon fiber frame led him to other exotic materials.

Gerald O'Donovan then did some work with *titanium*. Although he was able to solve the problem of how to braze the tubes together (titanium requires very special brazing techniques), he was prevented from producing many frames because of the component problem. Because of the large-diameter tubes required to compensate for titanium's "softness" (less "stiff" than steel), it is unsuitable for bicycle frames unless the component manufac-

Figure 9-1: Gerald O'Donovan (left) and one of the technicians discuss the setup of a frame prior to brazing.

turers redesign components that will fit the oversize tubes. In addition to the high cost of the titanium, there are design problems that must be solved before the frame can be manufactured. For example, if you have very large-diameter chainstays, how do you get the cranks to retain their normal width relationship without hitting the chainstays?

Unable to produce a titanium frame that would meet stiffness requirements, O'Donovan turned his attention back to steel alloys. In his search for lighter tubing, Gerald O'Donovan became involved with some work that was being conducted at TI Reynolds by Stan Smith, the chief metallurgist and Terry Reynolds, the technical director. They had discovered an interesting tube but they didn't know what to do with it. The problem, according to O'Donovan, was "How do we join it? How do we work with it?

Figure 9-2: One of the many Raleigh test machines. This machine measures the deflection of the bottom bracket under various loads.

What gauge should it be in? And how do we stress it? After all, how thick were we to make the tube walls?"

Working for more than two years, O'Donovan, in collaboration with TI Reynolds, developed what is now called Reynolds 753 tubing. Finally 753 tubing has emerged from the experimental into the trial stage. A lot of time and effort at TI Raleigh has gone into the development of 753, and Gerald O'Donovan is still continuing to change specifications for the 753 frames he is building to make the most out of this remarkable tubing.

Gerald O'Donovan believes that "everything on a frame ends up as a resultant of the *hanger* (bottom) *bracket*. No matter what you do. You stand on the pedal; you pull on the handlebar and it's transmitted through the frame to your foot." As a result of this belief, Gerald O'Donovan started off on the 753 project by doing stress analysis tests on the computer. By programming the stress requirements of the bottom bracket, he was able to work out the parameters of the loads resulting from pedaling, coasting, cornering, and braking. With the use of the computer, he was able to determine technical requirements of each of the frame's components.

Today, testing continues on 753 frames with sensors that register the stresses that are encountered during actual riding on the road. Concurrently, tests are performed in the laboratory at Ilkeston and at the TI Raleigh product testing center in Nottingham.

In one test, a complete bicycle is set up on a testing machine with 100 kilograms of weight distributed on the bicycle in a front to rear ratio of 45:55. Each wheel of the bicycle is placed on a test machine drum which simulates one of the worst types of road condition—Belgian cobbles. The bicycle is pounded for six to ten thousand miles at a simulated rate of 42 kph. After the bicycles have been run through a gamut of tests, they are cut up and examined.

At the Ilkeston factory there are only four builders, including Gerald O'Donovan, who are capable of building the 753 frames from start to finish. Production, if that's what you want to call it, can approach 10 to 15 frames per week but is usually far less. All the frames are silver-soldered since nothing else will work at the low temperature required for brazing 753. Mr. O'Donovan has spent years testing the mixture of the silver used and, understandably, he will not reveal its composition. He will only refer to it as "bullion, the stuff you keep in Fort Knox."

All tubes are held rigidly in jigs during the building of 753 frames. Once it's brazed, the frame cannot be bent into correct alignment. According to O'Donovan, "The problem with pulling frames before they're cool is that you tend to cause the copper in the brazing rod to run into crystalline joints of the steel that cause brittle and broken tubes. The prominent cause of broken fork blades, and they usually break at the top near the fork crown, is that the fork has been hot set."

The lugs that are used on the Raleigh 753s are generally made to O'Donovan's specifications by Raleigh, although he does use other makes such as Prugnat. Lugs are stocked in 72-, 73-, and 74-degree angles. These sizes will cover all the different angles used in normal 753 frame geometry. If a 75-degree angle seat lug is needed, it can be obtained from a 74-degree lug. O'Donovan believes that lugs are generally interchangeable within 1 degree. Reshaping a lug more than 1 degree is not possible because of the close tolerances required by the silver-brazing of 753. If the angle of the lug must be changed, it can be altered on a shaped mandrel to reduce any additional stresses on the frame tubes. Lugs must be tapered and not thinned all over. According to O'Donovan, if you file a lug to death and the mitering is off slightly, you've got a "mushy frame."

Since 753 cannot be hot set or cold set, there is usually little chance of getting it repaired properly in the event of an accident. Although 753 should not be reheated, it is possible to replace a chainstay without creating adverse effects on the rest of the frame. It is too "chancy" to replace any other tube. Remember this if you decide to order a custom-built 753 frame.

The care required in building with 753 is further demonstrated by the need to use chamfered (with brazed top plates) seatstays rather than a fastback stay. Gerald O'Donovan believes the smart builder is prohibited from attaching the seatstays to the seat tube since the seat tube is only .014 inch thick! He uses chamfered seatstays because the seat lug acts as a heat shield and minimizes the possibility of overheating.

Mr. O'Donovan's frame philosophy is that accuracy in building starts at the building stage, not after it's been made. "A frame should not be brazed to death, filed to death, and finished to death. Some builders have a very nice looking product, but by the time they're finished with it they've worked the poor frame to death before they've even started riding it. They've flogged it to death. We tend to go for a fair standard of finishing and a very great deal of engineering integrity."

Frame Selection

As O'Donovan continues to experiment with various designs for 753, he continually comes up against component problems. Presently, he is experimenting with TI Raleigh-manufactured lugs for some 753 frames, and he has also been able to arrange for a specification change on Campagnolo's titanium bottom bracket axle. According to O'Donovan, there is no relation between the titanium bottom bracket axles that the TI Raleigh team is using and the axles that are commercially available. The axles that O'Donovan has ordered are twice as strong because of their larger diameter. O'Donovan is a great believer in "reducing the gauge and increasing the section of the tubing." As a result, he believes that if further advancements are to be made in bicycle frames, component manufacturers are going to have to design new components to accommodate these various frame design improvements.

Gerald O'Donovan was a professional aircraft engineer during World War II and as a result was trained to think in terms of *ergonomics* in the design of equipment. He was required to translate the human body's motions into fixed distances. This training has carried over into his bicycle designs. Gerald O'Donovan personally designs the frames for the TI Raleigh team riders. He is the type of builder who can take a potential world champion and look at him and say "you need this type of bicycle for this event." Generally, before he designs a frame, he likes to see the rider in action. He likes to be able to observe his individual riding style because the "ideal" position for a rider from the ergonomic viewpoint may appear to be one position and the specific requirements for an individual may be quite different.

One interesting example is professional rider Hennie Kuiper who tends to ride in a more forward position than most people. Gradually, O'Donovan has adjusted the design of Kuiper's frame whereby the seat tube is set a little more forward than "normal." In general, O'Donovan is interested primarily in the rider's position on the bike. "I'm interested in where he is going to sit; the angles are where they fall." Perfect examples of this philosophy were the track bicycles O'Donovan built for Ferdinand Bracke, 1964 and 1969 world champion pursuit cyclist. They all had a 72-degree seat tube!

When building a custom frame, Mr. O'Donovan believes that the ideal frame should fit the rider without extreme adjustments of the component parts. In other words, if a rider has an ideal frame for his physique, the saddle should be centered on the seatpost and he shouldn't need to use a very long nor very short handlebar stem.

The 10-speed models that come to the United States are usually made at the Worksop factory. One-hundred eighty employees have the capacity to produce approximately 200 bicycles per day with Reynolds tubing. In reality, however, the factory produces only about 10,000 Raleigh 531DB bicycles a year. The Worksop factory is the only Raleigh facility that produces the Reynolds 531DB bicycles, the Reynolds 531 plain gauge bicycles, and some of those made from 2030 steel called "tp" or tube products-built bicycles. All of these bicycles are produced from standard specifications. Although the factory has the ability to produce one-of-kind custom bicycles, the majority of the custom frames are made for the Carlton–Weinman team. All team frames are hand-built to individual specifications.

On special request, you can have a Raleigh frame custom made by the Worksop factory. It is imperative that you go through the proper channels, however. TI Raleigh recommends that you pick an established Raleigh dealer who has the knowledge to match your individual measurements to appropriate frame dimensions. After the dealer has completed your order, he will send it to Raleigh Industries of America in Boston. They, in turn, will review your order and forward it to England. Once they receive the order in Nottingham, it will be sent to the engineering department where precise engineering plans will be drawn. The frame builders at the Worksop factory build only from engineering plans. Be prepared to wait from four to nine months for your custom frame. Generally, if you want a new custom frame for the upcoming bicycle season, Raleigh recommends placing the order one full season in advance.

Although most of us think of Raleigh as a good bicycle, few of us realize the efforts that have gone into their top-of-the-line equipment. In spite of growing inflation and demands to start mass production, they still maintain a sophisticated workshop that is unequalled in the world. Although they will not provide some of the services that make your bicycle visually unique, they can build a technically sophisticated frame that will equal the quality of the most famous custom builders.

CHAPTER 10

Woodrup Cycles

Woodrup Cycles
345-7 Kirkstall Road
Leeds LS4 2HD
England

Woodrup Cycles is a family business. The directors of the business are Stephen Maurice Woodrup (father), Stephen Woodrup (son), and Jean Woodrup (mother). The business started officially in 1952. Prior to that time Stephen Maurice, whom everyone just calls Maurice to avoid confusion with his son Stephen, was involved in a business partnership with another Leeds builder, Bob Jackson.

Background

When Maurice went into business with Bob in 1948, he was certainly not a novice. Maurice had been building frames for several years. He started building as a young boy in Keighley, a small town located 18 miles northwest of Leeds, in the 1930s. Here in Keighley, Maurice worked for a firm owned by Alex Shuttleworth who produced a frame called "Alworth." Maurice liked working for Shuttleworth, but he decided he would someday make bicycles for himself, with his name on them. He got the opportunity in 1948 when he started a four-year partnership with Bob Jackson.

After the dissolution of the partnership in 1952, Maurice opened up his own bicycle store. Together with his wife Jean, an avid cyclist herself who has held the ladies' national 10-mile record for some 15 years, they operated the bicycle store and in his spare time he would build frames. Business was good and it led to the opening of a second store in Leeds. Today there are two Woodrup Cycles—one on North Lane and one on Kirkstall Road.

The store on North Lane is managed and operated by Jean Woodrup. She sells the "bread and butter" machines—children's bicycles and utilitarian adult bicycles. Maurice manages the store on Kirkstall Road where you'll find a good supply of Woodrup framesets as well as various other makes of lightweight bicycles for touring and racing. Maurice does not build frames anymore but he does the finishing touches on all the top-quality bicycles, which includes cleaning out threads, building wheels, and checking for alignment.

The frame-building facility is located at the same address as the bicycle store on Kirkstall Road. It is to the rear of the shop and up a set of creaky, narrow stairs. In the frame-building shop there are three builders, and one apprentice, who produce from 400 to 500 frames per year.

Maurice and Jean's son is in charge of the frame-building shop. Stephen is a young frame builder of 30, but he is not an

Figure 10-1: Young craftsmen disassembling a damaged frame.

inexperienced builder by any means. Stephen has been involved with bicycles since the day he was born. Jean and Maurice regularly rode together and their newest addition joined the rides, at the age of six weeks, in a special sidecar attached to his father's bicycle. Since Stephen's first ride 30 years ago, he has ridden thousands of bicycles.

Stephen rides to work every day and also finds time for training. He is involved in racing in the Leeds area and finds that when he rides, whether it be to work, training, or in a race, he meets many riders on Woodrup frames. Jokingly he says, "We have to build them well, otherwise we'd find a customer running off the road because we ride so much." When Stephen refers to "we," he is referring to himself, his friend (and employee) Kevin Sayles, who is his regular cycling companion, and his parents.

The Woodrups are a cycling family. Maurice has been actively cycling for 45 years. In 1936, at the age of 17 he won his first race and although he was not able to pursue the sport he loves so much while in the army, upon his return he immediately started riding and has not missed a year since 1946. Both he and Jean can be seen every weekend with the Leeds Clarion Club, of which they have been members for 30 years, riding anywhere from 40 miles in the winter to 80 miles in the summer.

Building Philosophy

When Stephen left school, he thought he would try something other than frame building. He had spent practically his whole life in the bicycle store and he decided that he wanted a change. Having had some engineering courses while attending the College of Science and Engineering in Leeds, he found a position at Mountbank Sheet Metal Engineering Company, where he was exposed to industrial techniques in welding and design. Although he found the work fascinating, after six years he lost his enthusiasm for working for someone else. He decided that he preferred working with bicycles because it gave him more personal satisfaction and his hours were more flexible to do other things such as training and racing. Stephen returned to his father's shop.

Stephen's friend and riding companion, Kevin Sayles, helps Stephen meet the demand for the Woodrup frame. Kevin is only

21 but he has been building frames full time for six years. He started building frames for Bob Jackson, but now works for Stephen. He likes it better at Woodrup because the work isn't as regimented. It's more relaxing and easygoing. With the help of a couple of apprentices, Kevin and Stephen build around eight frames per week.

At Woodrup Cycles, they believe that it takes about six years to become an expert frame builder. "Frame building is mainly experience and it usually takes someone that long to be expert in the brazing and in design," claims Stephen. Since there are not a lot of books on the subject, expertise can come only through experience.

Like most custom frames, Woodrup frame tubes are mitered. The joints are tacked, but never pinned. Stephen believes it is an old-fashioned method that wastes time: "With a commercial frame builder, you've got to be able to do a good job, but you also have to be able to do it fairly quickly. Otherwise, you're just putting yourself out of the market." All the Woodrup frames are brazed with hand-held torches using Sifbronze. Since the Woodrups have been producing Reynolds 531SL frames, they have started using silver solder—but only on 531SL tubing. Stephen believes that there is no need to use silver on regular Reynolds 531DB and there is a disadvantage—additional cost. On the other hand, Stephen feels it is a necessity to use silver on Reynolds 531SL because of the lightness of the tubing.

Woodrup frames can be equipped with Italian section forks. These are generally requested on some of the better racing frames. Stephen doesn't believe that there is any real advantage in using the Italian fork sections: "People just like it better for style. They like the Italian look of frames which I personally do as well. I think some of the best builders in the world are Italians."

Most of the lugs used on Woodrup frames are Prugnat because so many people request them; however, Woodrup Cycles have the Roto cast lugs available which Stephen says "are a nicely finished-off lug set. They are stronger. They are stylish as well as make a nice frame." They also use a lot of the Cinelli fully sloping crowns as well as the Cinelli semi-sloping crowns (which Stephen prefers because of their superior finish). He believes both crowns are very strong but that the fully sloping is the stronger of the two. However, the excessive weight of the latter becomes a disadvantage in frames where the customer is interested in light weight. All bottom brackets in Woodrup frames are stamped steel, although Stephen would like to use cast bottom brackets. So far he has been unable to find one with English threading that is acceptable to him. He feels, however, that with the constant improvement of the cast products, he will soon be able to offer a Woodrup frame with cast lugs, fork crown, and bottom bracket.

Frame Selection

The Woodrup brochure describing the models that they produce indicates that they only build racing frames. This is not true. The brochure, according to Stephen, only indicates the variety of things they can do. They tend to make more racing frames, but that is only because of the influence the Woodrup name has in various clubs in the Leeds area. In fact, in the early 1960s, Woodrup and Ovaltine cosponsored a professional team.

The Woodrup philosophy in designing a touring frame is only to alter the angles and lengthen the wheelbase. The length of the top tube and seat tube should remain the same as if the person was being fitted for a racing frame. Stephen believes that positioning is an individual thing and that if a rider gets his position right, it should be varied only slightly for different events.

The alteration of angles from a racing frame to a touring frame will automatically, however, change the position of the tourist slightly. By reducing the angle of the seat tube, the rider will automatically be sitting behind the bottom bracket a little further.

Woodrup Cycles offers a full range of seatstay attachments: fastback, semi-wrap, and full wrap. Their most popular model is a version of the semi-wrap which is made out of the seatstay tops. They also do what Stephen terms "the ordinary semi-wrap" which uses a solid *top eye*. Stephen believes that top eyes are heavy and old-fashioned, but certain customers request them. As far as strength, Stephen doesn't think that there is much difference in any of the attachments as long as they have been fastened and brazed properly. Time trialists, he thinks, prefer the fastback stay because it looks faster and sleeker but unfortunately many of the fastbacks require a heavy insert to give them that sleek, fast look—contrary to what the time trialists actually need.

Many people in the bicycle industry consider the chrome

plating and paint jobs on Woodrup frames as good as any available. It is surprising to find that both the painting and the chroming are subcontracted. The frame workmanship is consistently clean and professional since the Woodrups believe in producing top-quality products. Their philosophy is best expressed by Stephen:

> We try hard, not for numbers particularly, but we try and give quality frames. We're all interested in cycling here. We're not building just for the cash really. We all race; we all ride the bicycle; we all mix with the people we're selling the frames to. We really take pains in making sure that our frames are good, all the way through, from the mitering of the tube to putting the transfers on at the finish. We try and make a first-class job of everything.

Part III

French
Frame Builders

In spite of the fact that France uses more Reynolds tubing than any other country in the world, the small French frame builders have not gained the popularity of the English or the Italians. Only the larger bicycle manufacturers like Peugeot and Gitane have gained any popularity in the United States.

French television is dominated by the many bicycle races that show the powerful and well-financed Peugeot and Gitane professional teams. Because of the strong exposure of "factory" frames, frame builders such as Routens, Limongi, Singer, Herse, and Fletcher produce excellent bicycles without a great deal of recognition or exposure.

Generally, the French place little emphasis on flawlessly painted frames. The French attitude on bicycles is one that values functionalism over aesthetics. More importance is placed on the quality of silk used in the tires for the bicycle than the quality of the paint on the frame. This attitude has not caught the fancy of the American market that sometimes overemphasizes the importance of a "perfect" paint job. The French philosophy can be paraphrased by the old adage, Don't judge a book by its cover.

An important consideration in selecting a French frame involves component selection. In most cases, you will be required to use French components on a French frame. The metric-size tubing that is used on most French frames requires a different-size handlebar stem and seatpost than the standard English/Italian sizes. All threads are French and they do not match the English- or Italian-threaded components.

French bicycles are well designed and built but have less attention to finishing details. Factory frames are very popular in France since they are functionally very similar to custom frames. As a result, there are proportionately less custom builders in France than there are in England or Italy.

CHAPTER 11
CNC Cycles

Fletcher–Laurent
Société Fletcher–Ducret
42, Boulevard de Bercy
75012 Paris
France

Société Fletcher–Ducret is a bicyle firm owned by Raymond Fletcher. It is based in Paris, where many of the bicycles are assembled, but the bicycle frames are built just outside Paris at Vitry. The reason for the split in facilities is due to Parisian city codes which do not allow industrial welding within the city limits.

The offices of Fletcher–Ducret are located in an old Parisian house not far from the Seine and within walking distance of the subway stop, Porte de Bercy. Next door to the main entrance is a series of connecting buildings where the bicycles are assembled, packed, and labeled for delivery throughout Europe.

Although the company is virtually unknown in the United States, it is fairly large and employs about 63 people. Mr. Fletcher builds bicycles under the names of Thomann, Chaplait, and CNC. The majority of the bicycles built are generally classed as utilitarian and children's bicycles. Although the CNC name is not well known in the United States, it has gained an excellent reputation in Europe. The CNC bicycles that Mr. Fletcher builds are top-quality racing machines. According to Eddie Borysewicz, American national cycling coach, it is very common to see some of the best Eastern European and Soviet bicycle riders using CNC bicycles. For 20 years Mr. Fletcher has been supplying the Eastern bloc with CNC racing bicycles.

Of the 63 people who work for Société Fletcher–Ducret, only five are allowed to build the good-quality frames. Of the five, only three are allowed to build the frames for the top-line CNC bicycle. The senior frame builder at Fletcher–Ducret has been there for 25 years. Previously he was outranked by an elderly gentleman of 82, whom Mr. Fletcher refers to as "the best frame builder in all of France."

Mr. Fletcher supervises the building of frames. At one time he built the frames himself, but today at the age of 70, he relies on other workers whom he has taught the "Fletcher way" of frame building.

Mr. Fletcher started building frames in 1936. His interest stemmed from the racing and touring he did early in his career. Up until 1976 Raymond Fletcher was racing in a French veteran's class, but his doctor compelled him to stop because of eye problems.

Today Raymond Fletcher beams with pride when mention is made of the firm he has built up in the last 40 years. The quality bicycles he builds are simple, functional, well-built machines. He

Figure 11-1: Raymond Fletcher and his four-legged assistant Viko in the hectic shipping area at Société Fletcher–Ducret.

prides himself with the fact that he has been building with Reynolds 753 for almost two years and has not encountered any problems.

At Fletcher–Ducret, frames are custom-built to individual specifications. A touring as well as a racing model can be ordered. But, like most European builders, they believe that a touring frame requires fenders and clincher tires, so that if neither of these are desired, it becomes essential to let the builder know.

The differences between the touring and racing models that Raymond Fletcher builds are characteristic of differences between most touring and racing frames. The racing frame has more upright angles, with a shorter wheelbase. Mr. Fletcher, however, is not very happy with some of the trends in racing frames. The angles, he claims, have become too steep in some cases, especially two years ago when the French riders wanted very upright frames. This, Mr. Fletcher believes, created an unstable bicycle, one that would not ride straight when you took your hands off the handlebars or one that would shimmy when going downhill. This has become a significant problem as builders have taken designs appropriate for one specific racing event and tried to make them universally applicable.

All the bicycles built by Société Fletcher–Ducret are brazed with hand-held torches. Brass is used on all the frames except for the Reynolds 753 for which a special silver solder is used. Lugs are stamped steel and fork crowns are cast. Only Reynolds tubing is used. Mr. Fletcher has indicated that he has been tempted to try Columbus tubing but his many years of success with Reynolds has limited his experimentation.

For some unknown reason, this firm has gained very little popularity in the United States. It is interesting that many of the builders interviewed throughout Europe had a great deal of respect for Mr. Fletcher's bicycles. He is regarded as one of the few French builders who understands both the technical procedures for building and the art of properly designing a frame for a rider's individual needs.

There are two primary reasons why the CNC frames have not gained popularity in the United States. First, the language barrier in dealing with a non-English speaking country appears to be more pronounced in France than in Italy. Second, the French utilitarian frames that are well constructed but not flashy, do not have the visual appeal that is so important in the United States.

CHAPTER 12

Cycles Gitane

Cycles Gitane
S.A. MICMO
44270 Machecoul
France

Cycles Gitane is located in Machecoul, a small town 40 kilometers south of Nantes in Brittany. Machecoul is somewhat isolated as there is no train service to Machecoul. From Nantes there is a commuter bus that leaves at around five o'clock in the afternoon. The same is true on the return trip, except that the bus leaves Machecoul early in the morning.

The Gitane factory has an overall production capacity of 750 to 800 bicycles per day. Total production for 1977 was one hundred-seventy thousand with an estimated two hundred thousand for 1978. This makes Gitane the third largest bicycle manufacturer in France.

Cycles Gitane employs about 525 people in the plant and around 80 in the offices. It is almost completely owned by Renault (98 percent), and its history is sketchy as a result of inadequate records and several changes of ownership. Still, Gitane's reputation for building quality bicycles remains.

Originally, Gitane was a small agricultural machinery shop which started assembling bicycles in 1920. The first frames were manufactured in 1925. Top-line Reynolds frames were made before World War II, but not until the 1950s were they made systematically on a large scale.

Today, all the Reynolds frames are brazed by hand-held torches. The people at Gitane feel that it is the best method to use. Since the control of the temperature is critical, the Gitane builders use hand-held torches rather than an automatic brazing oven.

The design of the top-line Gitane bicycles is relegated to a separate engineering department consisting of seven people. This department has the responsibility for designing and testing prototypes and engineering them for production. Components that are found on Gitane bicycles are also tested here. Input required in the final design of a Gitane frame comes from various places. It may come from an individual engineer or from someone in the commercial department who knows what the dealers will buy. The majority of the changes come as suggestions from the manager of Gitane's professional team as well as the individual team members.

Gitane considers their racing line to be very similar to their professional line. Response from the team is highly regarded by the Gitane engineers who feel the professional riders are sensitive to the problems with any Gitane product. The racing professionals are living so close to their bicycle that they can sense insignificant subtleties in a frame which would go unnoticed by the average cyclist.

According to Paul Chenevier at S.A. MICMO, production Gitanes are engineered as a compromise, just like a suit which has to be adjusted to each individual person. The engineers choose various compromises between the height and the length of the frame that are sometimes dictated by bicycle "fashion trends." One good example is the present trend to build frames with shorter top tubes. Gitane did not change their design since they have been consistently building frames with short top tubes since 1972. Mr. Chenevier claims that it is important to remember that many of the differences between builders are only based on habit or the builder who says "I know how to do it," but is unable to explain why.

While the cycling fashions change, these changes usually do not affect the fundamental characteristics of the frame. At Gitane they believe that technically, most frame building is generally based on habits which have never been questioned or reinforced by fundamental studies made by medical people. Chenevier believes that Gitane is leading the large manufacturers in a new approach—an ergonomic analysis of bicycle frame design.

In the spring of 1977 Gitane began an analysis of the current practice of custom frame design. To date, Gitane does not know what kind of results will be forthcoming or if there will even be any significant changes, but since very little research has been done in this area, Gitane feels confident that their results will be helpful with future bicycle designs.

Only one frame builder, who has been specifically trained as a brazing specialist, is allowed to build the custom Gitane frames. As of now, Gitane does not have a specific department that builds custom frames. Their production of custom frames is limited to the demands of their team riders. Gitane is, however, planning to develop a department which would be able to build custom frames on a regular basis for all their customers.

Gitane believes that the success of a frame depends on how well it is brazed. Mr. Chenevier says that 90 percent of the success of a frame, from the technical point of view, is the brazing.

The Gitanes are all brazed with a product called *Brox*, the French equivalent of bronze, or the English Sifbronze. The frames are brazed together on jigs and the tubes are held together initially with pins. Some of the lower end frames are *spot-tacked*, but this operation, even on the lower end frames, is being replaced with pinning. Seventy-five percent of the Gitane bicycles are pinned. All the lugs are made of stamped steel. However, Gitane has switched to a new semi-sloping cast fork crown.

Gitane uses only Reynolds tubing, although they are planning on expanding their line by producing a model with *Super Vitus* tubing. Mr. Lory, a Gitane technician, says that Gitane had thought about using Columbus but dropped the idea because of added costs created by what Mr. Lory called "added expenditure on component parts inherent only with Columbus tubing." Gitane is hopeful that it will soon be able to offer frames with Reynolds 753 tubing.

Although Gitane does not build custom frames for the average consumer, they offer a product that fills the need of the short person. The Tour de France and Super Corsa models in the past have always offered a well-made Reynolds 531 frame in the 19½-inch size. Combined with the short top tube, these bikes provide a good alternative to a custom-made frame for those persons who cannot fit many other production framesets.

CHAPTER 13

Cycles Peugeot

Cycles Peugeot
251, Boulevard Pereire
75852 Paris Cedex 17
France

Cycles Peugeot is a large con-
glomerate whose facilities are
spread throughout France. The
main offices are located in the
northwest section of Paris and the
primary manufacturing section is
located in the region of France called "Le Doubs." There is a
factory in Romilly which mass-produces "stock" bicycles. There
are also plants that are part of Cycles Peugeot which produce such
varied products as kitchen furniture, retail store equipment,
shelving units, containers, and car parts.

Cycles Peugeot was founded in 1926. Peugeot bicycles, however, were being made as early as 1885 when the original Peugeot
company, Les Fils de Peugeot Frères, started mass-producing
bicycles. The first Peugeot bicycles were built at the mill of Belieu
in the Beaulieu area of the Le Doubs region. The mill previously
had been producing wires for hoopskirts, but by the end of the
nineteenth century the hoopskirt was out of fashion. Bicycles,
however, were just beginning to gain in popularity. In response to
the change in demand, the mill of Belieu was transformed from
crinoline to bicycle production.

Today, Cycles Peugeot's buildings occupy thousands of
square feet in Beaulieu, a 45-minute drive from Belfort, the largest
city in the region. The bicycle division is one of the larger
divisions of Cycles Peugeot located in Beaulieu. This large complex houses a number of other divisions and departments.

The research and development department is located in
Dijon, but there is also a research department in the Beaulieu area.
Designs originate in Dijon and they are sent to Beaulieu where
they are modified. The research department in Dijon designs
prototypes and works with the production department in

eliminating any manufacturing problems. The research department in Beaulieu is also responsible for the assembly and adaptation of various models for different foreign markets. For example, the United States Consumer Product Safety Commission's standards are studied and modifications are designed and incorporated into already existing models.

Background

The research laboratory and the quality control department are both located in the same complex in Beaulieu. Both these departments work very closely with the research department in testing and analyzing both raw materials and finished products. These departments are vital in an operation of this size where so many different sources of materials are used in production.

Bicycle, moped, and car components are made by the general products department. Machines and tools are made for use in production by the machine and equipment department. Tube production is relegated to the tube production division where they make tubes for bicycles, mopeds, and car products. The stamping press division manufactures various parts and components and the plating workshop plates components with nickel-chrome at the rate of ten thousand square meters per month.

Cycles Peugeot's bicycle production at Beaulieu can be divided into three categories. The first is called total mass production—only one size is available in each model. All of these frames are automatically brazed on electrically charged brazing machines.

Racing-style bicycles are all hand-brazed by specially trained craftsmen. This area is a kind of semi-mass production operation. Everything in this area is hand-brazed on individual brazing stands. Each craftsman works according to engineering drawings and all the jigs are adjusted to accommodate the specifications of the particular frame. When working with Reynolds 531DB tubing, one worker spot-tacks the main triangle and then another worker brazes it. When brazing Reynolds frames, the temperature is usually from 600 to 700°C. (1,112 to 1,292°F.). All the frames in this area are brazed with Brox, which is the French equivalent of Sifbronze.

The third type of bicycle production at Beaulieu is done in the Prestige frame shop. Created in 1974, this area employs eight craftsmen and a foreman, Raoul Jeand'Heur. Monsieur Jeand'Heur has been working with the quality Peugeot bicycles since 1957. Prior to 1957 he was a teacher at Peugeot's mechanics' school, where he taught skilled trades to workmen in the bicycle and car industry.

Today, the Prestige frame shop builds frames for the professional Peugeot team and special customer one-of-a-kind orders. This specialty shop is equipped to build the frame as well as totally assemble all the necessary components to make a complete bicycle. Although this department has the ability to assemble components on the frames, only custom orders are assembled here. The Peugeot team frames are assembled in a special workshop in Paris.

The bicycles that are built in the Prestige area all use Reynolds tubing. The gauge differs according to the desires and needs of the customer. Generally, only frames using .3- and .5-mm.-thick Reynolds 531 tubes are used, but there are some unusual cases where they do use .7-mm. tubing. The .7-mm. tubing is generally only used in the semi-mass production area.

All the frames built in the Prestige frame shop are built from special drawings supplied by the research department. When a customer sends in his measurements, they are analyzed by the research department at Beaulieu. They believe that the frame size will usually correspond to about 9 inches (23 centimeters) less than the rider's inseam. According to Peugeot, this measurement should be taken with the rider's feet 10 inches (26 centimeters) apart. This usually determines the size of the frame and the other specifications are determined according to the specific needs of the rider. Generally, consideration on different top tube lengths is given to the professional team riders only.

Standard sizes range from 52 to 64 cm. Other sizes can be built, but usually the customer is dissuaded from ordering a frame smaller than 52 cm. or larger than 64 cm. because of the prohibitive cost of manufacturing.

The customer who orders a specialty bicycle from Peugeot has a number of options from which to choose. Usually, there are about five different colors, including both standard and iridescent finishes. A customer can order a frame with .5-mm. Reynolds 531 tubing or opt for .3 mm. at an additional cost. Also at extra cost, Peugeot will paint the owner's name on the frame or install a lightweight *headset, freewheel,* rims, seat, bottom bracket set, and derailleurs. At no extra charge, there is a choice of certain black *anodized* parts like pedals, derailleurs, and handlebars. The customer is also requested to choose the specifications for the freewheel and chainwheel as well as the size of the *crankarms,* handlebar stem, and *toe clips.* There is even a choice between low-flanged and high-flanged Maillard hubs. Choice of components continuously changes as a result of fashion; however, it is always restricted to specific French manufacturers. Nevertheless, the selection is varied and generally extensive enough to suit most needs.

Building Philosophy

When a builder receives an order for a custom Peugeot, he receives a drawing from the engineering department with it. The frame builder's job is to build according to the specifications provided. His task is to miter the tubes, file the lugs, tack, and finally assemble the frame. All the frames in this area are brazed with hand-held torches containing propane and oxygen or acetylene and oxygen. Brox is the brazing substance used, with silver used occasionally in brazing water-bottle holders on the down tube. Nervex stamped steel lugs are employed. Bottom bracket shells are also stamped steel but can either be Agrati or Nervex. Fork crowns are French cast semi-sloping.

Once the frame is brazed, it is checked against the drawing. If it meets all specifications, it is filed and then sent to the paint department. Once in the paint department, the Prestige frames and forks go through the pickling tanks rather than through a sandblasting process to clean them off. They are then coated with phosphate which insures that the paint will adhere to the metal. All the frames get a coat of anticorrosion primer and two coats of paint.

The painting and undercoating are done by an electrostatic process. The frame and forks are all hung on a conveyor belt and are carried through an electrostatic room where they are automatically painted. For each coat, including the undercoating, the frames first go through the automatic electrostatic paint room and, when they emerge, they are touched up with hand-operated paint spray guns.

The undercoating is baked for three minutes, the topcoat for 20 minutes, and the varnish coat for 20 minutes. The frames then go to the decoration department, where the transfers are applied. Application of the Peugeot decals requires a water solution comprised of 16 percent solvent. This solution aids the decal in adhering to the varnish-coated frame. If there is any *pinstriping* to be done, it is done by hand.

This entire process from pickling tanks to pinstriping is used on all frames except those built by the Prestige frame shop. The pickling process is the same, but the paint process differs in that all operations are performed in individual spray booths with hand-held spray guns.

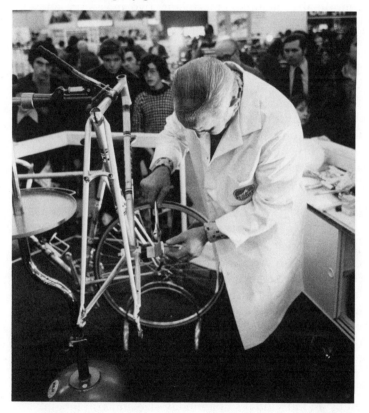

Figure 13-1: The man with the responsibility of keeping Thevenet's bicycle in perfect shape, Monsieur Raymond Valance. He has worked as a Peugeot team mechanic for 18 Tours de France!

Once the frames are painted, they are sent to the assembly area if they are mass or semi-mass production frames, or if they are custom frames, they are returned to Mr. Jeand'Heur's Prestige frame shop. Here, the bicycle is assembled with the components specified by the customer. If the frame is one that has been built for a Peugeot team member, it is returned to the Prestige shop only to be forwarded to Paris for assembly.

All components used on all the Team Peugeot bicycles are French. The team bicycles are assembled in Paris by the team mechanics who make all the final adjustments for each individual rider. These team mechanics not only initially make all the adjustments on team bicycles, but they also form part of a support staff which minimally includes one doctor, two masseurs, and two mechanics.

Monsieur Raymond Valance is one of Peugeot's team mechanics. He has been on 22 Tours de France, 18 of which have been for Team Peugeot. He personally works on Bernard Thevenet's bicycles, and together with another Team Peugeot mechanic in Paris, assembles all the team bicycles. One interesting note: When we saw Monsieur Valance set up a new bicycle for Thevenet, all the components and all the tools used to install the components were French. The bearings, however, were packed with Campagnolo grease!

Frame Selection

The research department engineers the frames for the team and the one-of-a-kind frames that are built for the customer. These frames differ from the semi-mass produced ones in that they are designed and custom-built.

Monsieur Yves Saugier is the section head of the bicycle technical research department in Beaulieu. His department is responsible for the final designs on all Prestige frames. These designs are translated into engineering specifications that are used by the frame builders in Monsieur Jeand'Heur's department.

In Saugier's department the top tube dimension of the frame is determined by an individual's upper body size and arm length. In designing standard semi-mass produced frames, a general rule is to base the top tube length on the "average" person. This is commonplace throughout the bicycle industry, but at Peugeot they don't like to vary the top tube very much on Prestige bicycles because they feel it upsets the balance of the bicycle's design.

Currently, custom frame requests sent to Mr. Saugier specify very short wheelbase bicycles. If they were to design many of these with the requested short top tubes, people would be hitting their toe clips on the front wheel when turning. For the professional rider, this is generally not a problem, but for the everyday cyclist it can be. Usually Saugier does not receive very many requests for extra-long top tubes, which, like the short top tubes, can also affect a balanced frame design. For this reason, before the frame is manufactured, an analysis would be performed to determine the effect of a long top tube on the overall responsiveness of the bicycle.

The design is always affected by style. Presently, almost all Prestige orders received are for short chainstays. Most professional riders request the shortest possible chainstays and the smallest frame possible. Frequently, riders select a frame that years ago would have been considered too small for their physique. The popularity of the "small" frame is simple; the smaller frame is usually stiffer.

The ideal design that Saugier and his colleagues use for the professionals is composed of 73- to 73.3-degree angles. They then vary the fork rake and the *caster* for the use of the bicycle. Usually a professional racer will have several bicycles and if possible will have a bicycle with a 30- to 35-mm. caster for climbing compared to a 75-mm. caster for downhills.

Although the shorter wheelbase gives a stiffer ride, there have been problems with high-speed handling, particularly when descending large mountains. To remedy this, Peugeot supplies the team riders with bicycles that have a greater degree of caster for long mountain stages.

At Peugeot, they believe that the caster determines steering ability and stability at high speed. The caster dimension can be increased in basically two ways: by decreasing the head angle or increasing the fork rake. According to Saugier, the ideal for the team professionals is to have 73-degree parallel angles which give the ideal length top tube (this refers to standard-size frames—not the smaller or the larger frames). This is ideal when combined with a fork rake of 35 mm. and a caster of 70 mm. This design is specifically intended for racing, however.

French builders seem to place less emphasis than the British or the Italians on the appearance of a frameset. Although the frames are well constructed, less time is spent on elaborate paint jobs and minor detail items. In spite of increased demand for "small," short-wheelbase frames, it appears that the French, in general, design frames that are larger and have longer top tubes than those found in England and Italy. Although Peugeot has a large and successful racing team, the factory seems less technically innovative than some of the other larger factories, such as Raleigh. If their response to a custom frame order equals the cooperation extended to us during our interview, the customer should feel confident that Peugeot will build a solid, quality product that should provide many years of satisfactory use.

PART IV

Italian
Frame Builders

Italy has become known as the home of cycling, a place where you can buy everything you'll ever need for riding. Everything from *spoke nipples* to the machinery used to manufacture them can be found in Italy. The Italian frame builder has become an innovator and leader in frame design since he works closely with the component manufacturers in designing prototypes. When a component manufacturer, such as Campagnolo, releases a new product, you can be sure the Italian frame builders have been using it for months.

The Italian frame builder is unique in the world because of his close association with the riders and coaches. They work collectively to optimize cycling efficiency. Frequently, the builder has had personal racing experience, but, unlike his British counterpart who was a time trialist, the Italian builder met with success in international *mass-start races*. Consequently, he is able to understand the needs of bicycle racers.

On the other hand, the Italian builder does not recognize the need for lightweight touring frames. In fact, we were unable to find any custom Italian touring bicycles. Although Italian frames may be used for touring, their builders are generally too involved in racing to devote any time to the design requirements of the tourist.

Italy has a disproportionately high share of the world's master builders. Some of the most revered builders (Cinelli, De Rosa, Pogliaghi, Colnago, and Masi) are Italian. Almost every little hamlet in Italy has its own frame builder.

The Italian builders are the most style conscious of all builders. They are interested in producing a frame that is aesthetically pleasing as well as functional. Their frames incorporate the latest examples of design theory. Like the famous Italian sports cars, the bicycle frames are built to look as fast as they perform.

The high-quality Italian frames are usually built with Columbus tubing because of the proximity to the Columbus factory and, in part, because of their strong sense of patriotism. All frames are built to accept Campagnolo components.

CHAPTER 14

Cinelli Cino & C.

Cinelli Cino & C.
Via Egidio Folli 45
Milano 20134
Italia

Cino Cinelli is 61 years old and his interest in bicycles has spanned almost half a century. Cino was born in 1916 in a small farmhouse just outside Florence in the province of Tuscany. He was the seventh of 10 children raised by Enrico Cinelli and his wife Marianna Banolli. Cino spent his early childhood on his parent's farm which included 36 square quadrameters of land devoted to growing grapes for chianti and olives for oil.

For the average Italian in the late 1920s, there were only three means of transportation from the countryside to the city: by foot, horse, or bicycle. Traveling by foot was too slow, and owning a horse was too expensive for the everyday farmer. Naturally, the bicycle became the most popular means of transportation. Cino got his first bicycle in 1929 when he was 13 years old. In those early days, Cino would ride to school in Florence with his brothers and sisters. Unfortunately, this was a difficult economic time for both Italy and the Cinelli family. Their modest farm could not support the large family and the older children had to quit school and go to work.

Arrigo and Giotto got jobs working in a bicycle store. Although it was a small store, the owner was an artisan who specialized in building racing frames. Arrigo's enthusiasm for his job spread throughout the family. Frequently, Cino would accompany his brother to work just to be able to look at the bicycle equipment.

In spite of the scarcity of jobs, Cino was lucky and got a position with a publishing firm in Florence, near the store where Arrigo worked. Once again Cino was able to ride with his two brothers Arrigo and Giotto, just like they had done while going to school. Their natural competitive spirit changed their commuting miles into three-man races held every day to, and from, work. This was the beginning of a career that would take Cino from commuter to professional bike rider, from unknown frame builder to manufacturer of some of the most respected bicycles and bicycle components in the world.

As the oldest of the Cinelli brothers, Arrigo started racing first. Giotto, and then Cino, soon followed. The Cinelli brothers did not have an easy time of it since their father vehemently disapproved of their bicycling activities. He thought that his sons would be better off spending their time in other more accepted, as well as more profitable, sports like horseback riding or target shooting. Although the brothers respected and feared their father, they were determined to become champion bicycle riders.

Background

Their refusal to accept their father's advice demonstrated their strong will and determination. Although their father was a fair and honest man, the people throughout Tuscany feared him because of his great strength. This fear stemmed from Enrico Cinelli's almost miraculous transformation from a frail child to a strong adult. Cino's respect for his father was obvious as he related this story, which was interrupted by fits of laughter.

When Enrico was a young child, his mother became so concerned over his poor health that she consulted a doctor for help. The doctor's advice was unorthodox, but she blindly administered the prescribed "cure." The doctor had advised her to feed Enrico a bowl of soup "fortified" with iron shavings! Enrico ate this soup every day for three years and became one of the strongest men in Tuscany. His daily consumption of iron filings became legend and he became known as the "iron man."

Arrigo raced for two years in the amateur class and discovered that he wasn't as good as he thought. He had visions of winning the Giro di Lombardia, but had difficulty winning local races. Unlike Arrigo, Giotto began winning many of the races he entered. As Giotto started winning races and became a local hero, it was difficult for Enrico Cinelli to forbid his sons to race. Although Enrico never fully sanctioned his sons' racing, he became proud of their achievements.

Cino started racing in the junior category at the age of 15. Like

Giotto, he won many of the races he entered. Cino was not a very muscular youngster and many people believed that he would never be a top-caliber rider. Some thought that his physique would limit him to becoming a gregario (a rider who is not paid to win but instead is paid to support a selected member of a team). Cino's determination and training paid off because each year he became stronger, more confident, and won more important victories.

In 1935, when Cino was 21 years old, he entered the senior amateur category. At this time he was still working in the publishing business. Fortunately, his employer was good to Cino, allowing him to work only half days so that the remainder of his time could be devoted to training. A major change in Cino's life occurred when his boss was replaced. His new manager gave Cino an ultimatum: work or train. Since his winnings had been providing enough money to live on, Cino chose to make his livelihood from his greatest love: cycling.

Cino became the hope of Tuscany with Giotto's retirement. Cino won so many races as an independente that he was practically forced into becoming a professional. Lucrative professional offers came quickly. Cino rode for Frejus in 1938 and 1939; and for Bianchi from 1940 to 1943. Cino won many of the great Italian classic road races: the Giro di Lombardia, the Giro di Piedmont, the Giro di Campania, and the Milan–San Remo. These victories were major accomplishments since Cino was riding with some of the greatest racers of all time—Gino Bartali and Fausto Coppi, to name only two.

When World War II broke out, Cino was required to join the army. Mussolini shared his country's love of cycling and the bike racers were not sent to the war front. Instead, they remained in Italy and continued racing. Although the war reduced the number of races, they were no less competitive. Once Mussolini's Fascist government was overturned, bike racing activities came to an end until after the war. Cino officially retired from racing in 1944, on the day he won the Milano–Varese stage race. His decision to retire had been partially affected by the damage the war had inflicted on his country. The track in Milan had been bombed to ruins and all road racing activity had virtually ceased with the invasion of the Allied forces. Although some local races were still held, all of the major races were canceled because of the increased war activity.

Building Philosophy

During his racing career he had become increasingly aware of the inadequacies of his racing bicycle. Cino did not resume his racing activity after the war like Bartali and Coppi; he had other plans. He became more contemplative than competitive. World War II created just the interruption needed to direct Cino's time and energy to activities other than training and racing.

During Cino's racing career he developed amiable relations with many people in the bicycle industry. He became acquainted with factory representatives as well as owners of bicycle factories, including Benotto.

During his employment with Benotto, Cino devoted his spare time to design improvements of bicycle frames and parts while his

Figure 14-1: The Cinelli workshop.

wife, Hedi provided administrative assistance. Unlike Cino, she was neat and efficient, and made sure that everything went like clockwork. They were a very complementary team. He provided the ideas spawned by his cycling passion and she assembled a business structure that brought his ideas to fruition. Their only child, Andrea, was born during this very busy time in their lives.

The first two years of the Cinelli business were not devoted to frame building or to the manufacturing of parts. Typical of Cinelli's usual thoroughness, two long years were devoted to the design of products that would be superior to anything currently available. If not, they would never bear the Cinelli name.

The first problem Cino set out to tackle was the lack of stiffness he had experienced in the bicycle equipment he used while racing professionally. Cino had developed into a powerful sprinter and was not satisfied with the products available at the time. They were not rigid enough. His concurrent goals were improved aerodynamics and reduced weight without decreased strength.

Although Cino was neither a mechanical nor a design engineer by trade, he had an innate talent that is hard to duplicate. He constantly discussed problems involving strength and aerodynamics with the experts of his time. Because of his enthusiasm and innovative ideas, they assisted him with the structural testing and the benefits of their formal education. Cino synthesized his racing experience with their technical opinions, and manufacturing began in 1947. Although he began producing custom frames at this time, his first real product was a set of lightweight-alloy handlebars that were almost as strong as the steel counterparts. His handlebars became the standard of the industry, and even today they are the first choice of virtually every bicycle builder.

Today, Cinelli Cino & C. occupies a group of small buildings at Via Egidio in an industrial section of Milan. Cino is still very fit and rides about 200 to 300 kilometers (120 to 180 miles) per week. Currently, Cino is riding his new prototype bicycle which will be covered in more detail later.

Cino Cinelli has not personally built bicycle frames since the early 1960s but he still supervises every single operation that is done by the two frame builders he employs. All the Cinelli frames are hand-built on the premises using acetylene and oxygen-fed hand torches. The demand for Cinelli bicycles is so great and their production capability is so small, that during an Olympic year, production only meets the demand of Olympic teams. Everyone else has to wait until the following year to put in their order. As a result of Cinelli's ability to understand the rider's needs, he had a virtual monopoly on track frames used from 1960 through 1970.

The Cinelli philosophy is to keep frame production at a level that will allow perfect quality control. In spite of the fact that Cinelli's are more expensive than even the most popular custom frames, Cino claims that his attention to detail results in every frame being sold at a loss! The majority of sales revenue comes from the sale of Cinelli lugs, fork crowns, bottom brackets, seats, handlebars, and stems. Cinelli Cino & C. would rather market their component parts because of the decreasing number of skilled workmen "willing" to build frames. Willing to Cino means more than just having the desire; the builder must work as if his name appeared on frame and not be working for the salary alone. Consequently, yearly production rarely exceeds 350 frames.

Many Cinelli innovations have become standards that are accepted by the bicycle industry. For instance, one of the first design changes Cino made on his bicycle was the fork crown. The Cinelli fully sloping crown was a revolutionary design in the 1940s since all the fork crowns in those days were flat. There are two advantages with the Cinelli fully sloping fork crown—superior aerodynamics and increased strength.

The reduced frontal area of the fully sloping fork crown results in less wind resistance—a factor that geometrically increases as speed increases. Moreover, the overall fork as a unit is more rigid with the fully sloping crown because the length of the fork blade is reduced. The solid cast crown is unexcelled for integral strength and when combined with the shorter fork blades, the combination is unsurpassed in rigidity, Cino's prime concern.

Frame Selection

Cinelli-style forks are usually preferred on frames where rigidity is more important than comfort. Cinelli further justifies the use of the crown by its relation to the frame. When building a fork for stiffness, he believes it must be in harmony with the rest of the frame. The forks must be as stiff as the main and rear triangles. No more, no less. There is little value in building a fork that is more rigid than the main triangle or rearstays since they will work at "cross purposes."

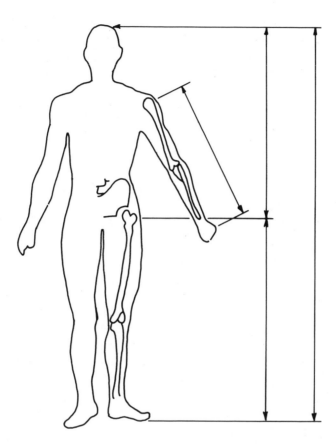

Figure 14-2: This is a copy of a card used by Cinelli to determine the measurements necessary to build a custom frame. Cino Cinelli is one of the few builders to use the distance from the head of the femur to the floor (in bare feet) as the principle measurement in frame design. This measurement is used instead of inseam measurement since it eliminates any inaccuracy caused by fat or muscle covering the pelvic bone. Depending on the body proportions of the individual, a basic guide for proper frame sizing is to subtract 32 to 34 cm. from the distance between the head of the femur and the floor. For instance, if the measurement from the femur to the floor is 93 cm., the correct size frame is between 59 to 61 cm.

All three main parts of the frame (the fork, the main triangle, and the rearstays) must work harmoniously and have similar properties of elasticity. When referring to elasticity in this context, Cinelli does not limit the term to flexibility. He includes the absorption of road vibrations by the entire frameset rather than by a specific part of a certain tube. The harmonious balance of the frameset is important because it contributes to the handling, longevity, and overall strength of the bicycle.

Cino believes that his fully sloping fork crown should be used only on relatively smooth surfaces. When using the fully sloping crown on the *pavé*, it will transmit a lot of frontal vibrations and adversely affect the rider. The rider will be forced into directing all his energies to keeping the bicycle going in the right direction and too much of his energy will dissipate as his body acts as a shock absorber. To compensate for the extreme stiffness of the Cinelli fully sloping crown, some builders increase the rake of the forks. Cino thinks this is inadvisable since a longer fork blade adversely affects stability. If a frame is to be used on predominantly smooth roads, a semi-sloping or fully sloping fork crown should be used. A flat or semi-sloping crown is recommended for rougher roads, since both these fork crowns will be able to better absorb road shock than the fully sloping crown.

The bicycles that Cino manufactured in 1947 have changed little in the past 30 years. Although minor improvements have been made, no major revisions have taken place. The head lugs are stamped steel, but the seat lug, bottom bracket, and the fork crown are castings. The frame angles have not been changed even though many other manufacturers have followed trends to build frames with steeper angles. Although all Cinelli frames are custom-built to precisely fit an individual rider's physique, the majority of the frames are built within definite parameters. These parameters represent the limits at which Cinelli feels a bicycle's performance and handling are not hindered. Generally, frames are built anywhere from 49 to 70 cm. Top tube length varies from 51 cm. on the 49-cm. frame, to 59 cm. on the 70-cm. frame. The seat angle seems to be an important consideration since it is the only angle that is consistent in every case. Seat angles on Cinelli frames vary from 71.3 degrees for six-day frames to 74.3 degrees for criterium road frames and track sprint frames. In 30 years, Cino has never been swayed by fads. He does believe, however, that "the bicycles that are produced now are good bicycles but they are the wrong bicycles for the good roads we have today.''

Cino believes that a new bicycle design is needed as the cobbled and bricked roads are being replaced by smoothly surfaced roads. His new design includes steeper angles, but he believes the design must incorporate smaller-diameter wheels to accommodate the steeper angles. Since the position of the rider must be altered, it is necessary to incorporate certain changes that will give the rider optimum efficiency. This is done by providing longer cranks (about 180 to 185 mm.) and raising the bottom bracket height. This, however, must all be designed to conform with Cino's smaller-diameter wheels, smaller rear triangles, and shorter forks. The reduction of the size of the components will, in simplest terms, increase the rigidity, aerodynamic efficiency, and stability of the modern bicycle.

According to Cino, the wheel size that riders are presently using was developed to traverse cobblestones. Smaller-diameter wheels were found to fall between the cobbles, created vibration problems, and tended to break easily. Large-diameter wheels (like the old *high-wheelers*) were unstable and aerodynamically ineffi-

Figure 14-3: The new, redesigned (and very expensive) Cinelli handlebar stem. The new design eliminates the traditional front bolt for tightening the handlebar. The removal of the bolt results in improved aerodynamics.

cient. As the cobbled roads in Europe disappear, a small wheel becomes an advantage for several reasons: decreased wind resistance, decreased rolling resistance, increased strength and rigidity. Cino believes that the optimum size of the wheel is approximately 26 inches (66.7 centimeters) and to prove his theories he has had special lightweight rims and tubular tires manufactured for his prototypes. As a result of the increased strength gained through the reduced spoke length, he has had special narrow hubs manufactured to further decrease wind resistance.

The new Cinelli frame is designed for the smoother road surfaces and the higher racing speeds of today. In 1925, the average speed maintained in a race was about 25 to 30 kph (15.5 to 18.6 mph). Now it's very common to maintain an average speed of 45 kph (27.9 mph). In order to continue to increase this average, Cino believes that bicycles require steeper angles, higher bottom brackets, revised positioning of the rider, longer crankarms, and smaller wheels. Cino has already built several prototypes that have undergone rigorous testing in Rome where various groups are evaluating the benefits of the bicycle on the performance of individual riders.

One of Cino's first prototypes was ridden by Ole Ritter in Mexico when he broke the hour record in 1968. The bike had the longer crankarms, special Campagnolo hubs (2 cm. narrower), special-size Clement tires and Nisi rims, and a special Cinelli fork (winged-shaped fork blades on top and rounded at the bottom). Although this new Cinelli design may someday be the norm, it will be some time before we see it on the road since it requires retooling by some of the major component manufacturers.

Cino Cinelli is a master frame builder who is unique in his innovative ideas. His most important asset is his ability to translate a rider's physical limitations into a frame that maximizes his strengths and minimizes his weaknesses. Every motion that a rider makes has been studied by Cino in order to extract useful information to incorporate in designing his framesets and parts. He constantly experiments and uses the advice of sports physicians, trainers, and engineers to develop his new products. Cino has devoted his lifetime to the sport he loves and he, and his products, are highly regarded throughout the world.

In Italy the name of Cinelli rings of magic. In the Italian cycling community, Cino Cinelli is considered the chief hierarch of racing bicycle builders. His advice is sought after by many other frame builders who lack the training to understand technical effects of changing their designs because of style.

The Italian bicycle racers, in particular, have a special fondness for Cino Cinelli. This relationship has developed beginning with his friendships with Gino Bartali and Fausto Coppi. The highly respected trio organized the Italian Professional Cycling Association for professional riders. The intent of the organization was to educate the riders of their rights and to represent their interests in the Italian Bicycling Federation as well as the Italian Sports Federation. Cino was president of the association for 24 years.

Finally, the book which most racers refer to as their "bible," the C.O.N.I. *Cycling* book, is based on many of Cino's ideas. It is a compilation of the wealth of ideas and experiences of Cinelli, and two highly respected Italian coaches, Rimedio and Costa.

CHAPTER 15

Guerciotti

Guerciotti
Via Petrella 4
Milano 20124
Italia

In 1962 the Guerciotti brothers, Italo and Paolo, started a small bicycle store in Milan. They brought with them many years of experience as riders as well as mechanics. Italo liked road races and *cyclo-cross*. His best performance was a first-place finish in the 1959 Italian cyclo-cross championships, sixteenth in the 1959 worlds, and thirteenth in the 1960 worlds. In 10 years of racing, Italo won approximately 100 races. As a professional team member, he rode in many of the Italian classics like the Milan–San Remo and the Giro di Lombardia.

Paolo followed in his older brother's footsteps and began racing in 1960. He won 80 road races before he retired in 1965 to devote more time to the growing business. Unable to shake the desire to race, he started to cyclo-cross in 1967. He is still competing, and in the past 10 years, Paolo has won 50 races in amateur cyclo-cross.

Background

The first few years at Guerciotti were devoted to establishing themselves in the community and to the planning and designing of the Guerciotti frames. These were hectic times since Paolo was still racing and, in order to keep their small business afloat, both Italo and Paolo were moonlighting as team mechanics. Italo had previously been a Cynar team mechanic and was able to secure positions for himself and Paolo as mechanics for both the Bianchi amateur and professional teams. Bianchi's decision to quit their sponsorship of racing teams in 1965 caused the Guerciottis to switch their emphasis to their store.

Building Philosophy

In 1965 the Guerciottis started building their frames as a full-time business. They hired their uncle Lino Tempesta, an experienced builder, to provide additional guidance. Lino had been building frames for Bianchi in Bergamo for 15 years. He knew how to "use a torch" and he was a superb artisan. Their uncle's experience alone was not enough for Paolo and Italo. Before Paolo and Italo started building frames, they sought answers to the many unresolved questions involving bicycle design theory. They were interested in building a quality product that would respond to the racers' needs. In order to do this, they sought additional technical advice from Cino Cinelli. Paolo says that, "Mr. Cinelli is a very important man in bicycling. He is very clever and knowledgeable in all aspects of frame building. Mr. Cinelli was very instrumental in getting us started in frame building." Cino Cinelli provided the Guerciottis with frame design theory, brazing techniques, and the secrets of assembling individual frame parts, like the proper fitting of the chainstays in the bottom bracket.

Combining the elements of experience from their bicycle racing, their tenure as team mechanics, Cino Cinelli's frame-building advice, and Lino Tempesta's frame-building experience, the Guerciotti frame was conceived. Today, almost 15 years later, the Guerciotti frame has established itself in the bicycle world. The demand is so great that the Guerciotti order form is printed in four languages: German, French, English, and Italian. Although Guerciotti is most popular in Europe, it is quickly gaining popularity in the United States. U.S. Olympic rider George Mount has owned several Guerciotti frames although they are hard to recognize since they are repainted with his club colors. George rode one of his Guerciottis to a sixth-place finish in the 1976 Olympic road race in Montreal.

Paolo, Italo, and Uncle Lino did all the frame building at their Via Petrella location. By 1972 the demand for Guerciotti bicycles had grown to the point where they had to recognize the fact that they needed to expand their manufacturing capacity. Even the bicycle store facilities were too small to accommodate the increased business that they were developing year by year. Fortunately, a larger location was available just around the corner on Via Tamagno. This location was large enough for an assembly area, but was not suitable for frame building since Milan's city code prohibits the use of brazing torches in a building that has tenants living in it. As a result, the Guerciottis decided to move their frame-building operation into a vacant house outside Milan. This

Figure 15-1: Paolo Guerciotti in a cyclo-cross race.

division in facilities still remains: the bicycle store at Via Petrella; the bicycle assembly area, quality-control area, offices, and small workshop at Via Tamagno; and frame building outside of Milan.

Paolo and Italo soon found that the ever-increasing popularity of their bicycle store and their small export business consumed the majority of their time; consequently, they were unable to build the frames themselves. However, Guerciotti frames are still being built by Uncle Lino. Lino supervises the three frame builders who are now working for the Guerciotti firm, and Paolo and Italo supervise the quality control and design of the frames. They are so concerned about their reputation that they personally assemble the complete bicycles themselves in their workshop on Via Tamagno.

Both Italo and Paolo strive for efficiency as well as quality in their business. For this reason they thoroughly check every frame to insure quality workmanship. In order to expedite the frame-building operation, all lugs and dropouts are uniformly filed and cleaned before they are sent to their frame builders. This enables a

Figure 15-2: One of the many small touches available for the Guerciotti owner—engraved handlebar stem.

builder to concentrate on the mechanics of building a frame. He does not have to concern himself with various miscellaneous problems that are unrelated to the actual building process. A Guerciotti frame builder's only job is to build frames according to the design specifications that they receive from Italo and Paolo. With every set of specifications, each frame builder receives a set of tubes, lugs, and ends which have already been cleaned and filed for building. The tubes are mitered and then the joints are spot-welded. After each joint is brazed with brass, the frames are cooled in the jig before filing.

Before the frame is painted, Italo inspects and double-checks it for alignment. If it meets Italo's approval, the frame is sent to the sandblaster and then to the chrome shop. All Guerciotti frames, unless otherwise specified, have chrome dropouts and a totally chrome right chainstay. These are nice features since most bicycles that are painted in these areas soon become chipped or scratched as a result of removing the wheels.

Once the frame is chromed, it is sent to the painter. After the frame is painted, it goes to the Guerciotti shop on Via Tamagno which now also serves as an assembly area. The frame is checked again for alignment before it is built up into a bicycle or packed for shipment. If the frame is used for stock, it is placed in the Guerciotti retail shop on Via Petrella.

All Guerciotti frames are built with a special, stamped steel bottom bracket that is specially designed and includes the Guerciotti logo—a star. The fork crown is a cast semi-sloping design with a large "G" cutout on the top. The seat cluster arrangement is a chamfered design. The finishing touch on the frame is the plate that is brazed onto the seatstay which has an engraved "Guerciotti" signature. After the frame has been painted, the signature on the seatstay plate is painted in a contrasting color.

Frame Selection

Paolo and Italo use Columbus tubing on all their frames for two reasons: first, the superb quality of Columbus tubing; and second, the Columbus factory is only three kilometers from their store. Guerciotti frames can be ordered with two different types of seatstay tubes. The first is the normal seatstay—small diameter on the dropout end which becomes larger as it goes up to the seat cluster. The second is a special Columbus design that has a small diameter on both ends which becomes progressively larger as it reaches the middle of the seatstay. The "normal" seatstay is generally exported to this country because of American tastes which tend to like the beefy, chunky-looking seatstays. There is, however, no difference in strength between the two; at least this is what A. L. Colombo and various frame builders have advised us. The difference is a matter of style, or according to Paolo—"aesthetics."

Guerciotti, like most Italian custom frame builders, only builds racing frames. The Guerciotti frame design is based on Italo's and Paolo's years of experience as riders. They build their medium-size frames (53 to 58 cm.) with a 73-degree seat angle and a 74-degree head angle. They feel this is the best frame design for optimum performance in stiffness and speed, both on the flats and in the mountains. This 73/74-degree combination gives the bicycle the flexibility it needs going up mountains and the stiffness it needs going around corners. Frames that are smaller than 53 cm., and larger than 58 cm., require a change in design. In these cases, the angles are revised to approximate the handling characteristics of the standard-size frames.

Usually a 63-cm. frame will have a 59-cm. top tube; a 65 cm. will have a 61-cm. top tube; a 49 cm. will have a 51-cm. top tube. These will vary, however, with the individual's measurements. According to Paolo, the most important feature in building a racing frame is to build every frame, irregardless of its other dimensions, with the steepest possible head angle within the limitations of good performance and good handling.

The Guerciottis custom-fit frames according to an individual's body measurements. To custom-build a frame, they need the rider's inseam measurement, outside leg measurement from the top of the femur bone to the floor in stocking feet, and the arm measurement from the shoulder to the knuckles. Once they have these measurements, they check them against their secret measurement chart to find the correct size of each frame tube.

Initially, Paolo and Italo kept a record of all the various individual dimensions and the frame sizes needed to accommodate these differences. After having custom-fitted thousands of frames, they were able to develop a fairly accurate chart. Today, however, the Guerciottis use a revised version of the measuring chart found on page 132 of the C.O.N.I. *Cycling* book.

Including all the frames that are built for the Guerciotti professional team, only about 600 Guerciotti frames are built each year. Paolo does not believe that any one Guerciotti frame is produced better than another. He says that "they are all the same. They must be brazed all the same." The Guerciotti you purchase is made to the same precise standards as those used by their professional team.

The Guerciotti should appeal to the racer who is interested in a modern top-quality racing frame that has been developed from years of racing experience. Italo and Paolo have successfully blended the conservative techniques of some of cycling's master builders with the innovations gained from their recent racing experience.

CHAPTER 16

Sante Pogliaghi

Sante Pogliaghi
Via C. Cesariano 11
Milano 20154
Italia

In the central section of Milan you will find the small frame-building shop of Sante Pogliaghi located near the Arco della Pace, a neo-classic arch similar in design to the Arc de Triomphe in Paris. Within walking distance is another Milanese landmark, the Castello Sforzesco. Many works of art are displayed in the castle, the most renowned being Michelangelo's Pieta. Amid all this history is a small unobtrusive shop whose address is Via C. Cesariano 11, but whose entrance faces Vaile Bryon indicated by the "Pogliaghi" painted above the door.

Sante Pogliaghi has probably been building bicycle frames longer than any other master builder. He is 62 years old and started building when he was 11! He worked with his Uncle Brambilla, a famous frame builder of the 1920s. When his uncle died in 1947, Sante Pogliaghi continued building frames but now they appear with the Pogliaghi label.

Pogliaghi builds primarily road and track racing frames. His specialty, however, is the competition tandem. The lugs on the Pogliaghi tandem are hand made by Pogliaghi himself. Since Columbus builds custom large-diameter tandem tubes for Pogliaghi, he is unable to use standard lugs since no one makes tandem lugs that meet his exacting specifications. Consequently, he makes them himself.

Pogliaghi has built a few touring frames and touring tandems, but these are not his speciality. He is much more familiar with the technical requirements for racing than he is for touring.

Today, Pogliaghi frames are famous throughout the world. Just a few years ago, this little shop built 100 to 120 frames per year. Now it produces about 800 to 900 frames in the same period.

There are six builders, including Pogliaghi, and each builder works on a frame from start to finish.

The frames are all hand-brazed without the use of jigs. To help keep the frame from moving, the joints are pinned. Pogliaghi does have a frame jig which he employs when he is building a lot of frames of the same dimensions, but he generally likes to work without a jig. He feels that since he has built frames for 50 years, he can build accurately without a jig. He also feels that when a jig is holding the tubes, the frame will have heat-induced stresses that can result in distortion after cooling.

Contrary to normal practice, he builds a frame by joining the seat tube to the bottom bracket and then the seat tube to the top

Figure 16-1: The workshop at Pogliaghi.

tube. When he finishes this, he attaches the down tube to the bottom bracket and finishes the main triangle by attaching the head tube.

For the individual framesets, Pogliaghi brazes with what he terms "the natural gas, the cooking one." He also uses propane gas, but only for the larger-diameter tubed tandems. He prefers natural gas because it has 10 percent carbonics. "And so the tube, when heated, loses 10 percent carbonics, but by using the natural gas you only lose 5 percent." Pogliaghi uses a Swiss product called *Castolin* to braze his frames. It is, according to Pogliaghi, a type of bronze rod. But it actually has a silver content of about 40 percent. Pogliaghi has tried using brazing materials with higher silver content but finds that they are too liquid to efficiently complement his building techniques. He is satisified with the results achieved by using Castolin since Castolin has high fluidity, a low brazing temperature, and good brazing resistance.

Pogliaghi does not design a frame to meet specific angles. He is more concerned with the length of the top tube in proportion to the seat tube. As a general rule of thumb, Pogliaghi will build a bicycle with a top tube only 2 cm. larger or smaller than the seat tube. Otherwise, the bicycle will be ill proportioned and will not ride correctly. For example, if you order a 58-cm. Pogliaghi, the top tube from the center of the head lug to the center of the seat lug, can vary from 56 to 60 cm. depending on your individual needs. However, this rule only applies to the medium-size frames. The small and the large frames will not follow this rule. For example, the smallest top tube Pogliaghi will put on a 47-cm. frame is 49 cm.

Pogliaghi does not use cast lugs or cast bottom brackets on his frames. He thinks that they create a frame that is too rigid and, as a result, prone to tube breakage at the joints. He does, however, use a cast fork crown, because he feels that the fork must be stiff in order to provide good handling. He generally builds with Columbus tubing, but he will build with Ishiwata or Reynolds tubes, depending on what the customer wants.

All Sante Pogliaghi's frames are sent out for painting and chroming. Sante Pogliaghi, however, cautions about chroming. He believes the chroming should not be done in a sulfuric acid base, otherwise it will eat away at the tube and eventually crack it. A word of advice from Pogliaghi if you must have your frame chromed: "Oil the inside of the frame after it has been chromed" to prevent rust.

In Italy, and especially in Milan, Pogliaghi is called the "master tailor of the bicycle." He has custom-fitted frames for many world-class riders like Sercu, Merckx, Fagin, as well as Italian champions like Baghetto, Nunzi, and Rossi. If you would like Pogliaghi to build a frame, you had better give him your order soon as he plans to retire by 1980. The process is somewhat difficult since Pogliaghi only speaks Italian. We recommend that you order a frame through one of the many bicycle stores throughout the United States that deal directly with Pogliaghi. Because of his ability to custom-design a frame to an individual rider's physique and racing speciality, there is a long waiting list for a Pogliaghi custom frame. Recognizing that not everyone will necessarily be interested in a Pogliaghi frame, Signore Pogliaghi recommends other Italian builders in Milan whom he believes are superb craftsmen: Cinelli and De Rosa.

PART V

American Frame Builders

With the exception of the Schwinn Bicycle Company, frame building is in its infancy in the United States. Most American builders have entered the profession within the last decade. With the exception of the European builders who emigrated to the United States (Colin Laing, who is English but builds in Phoenix, and Francisco Cuevas, who is Spanish but builds in New Jersey for Paris Sport), most are young. Few are over 30.

The Americans are considered technicians rather than artisans like the Europeans. Few European builders use lathes, mills, and jigs in the frame-building process. Because of American preoccupation with perfection, the American builder sometimes tends to overfile the frame to achieve flawless lugwork. Although he has far less experience than his European counterpart, the American builder compensates by being more innovative. Generally he will build any desired frame configuration and he does not limit himself to the use of only one kind of tubing. Instead, he finds use for Reynolds, Columbus, and Ishiwata tubing.

Finally, he is more tolerant of unusual requests such as 18-inch or 29-inch frames although some handling problems may result because of an untested or unsound design. Some of the less-experienced builders are so anxious to please their customers that they may construct a technically unsound frame.

The American frame builders will be a force to be reckoned with. Although the number of competent builders are few, their experience grows daily as the demand for their products increases.

CHAPTER 17
Schwinn

Schwinn Bicycle Company
1856 North Kostner Avenue
Chicago, IL 60639

When most Americans think of bicycles, they think of Schwinn. The Schwinn name has become synonymous with quality bicycles. Schwinn became a leader by providing expertly engineered bicycles backed by a generous manufacturing quality guarantee. People have claimed that Schwinn was the impetus behind the bicycle boom of the 1970s by promoting and introducing strong and reliable 10-speeds with stem shifters and dual brake levers. Whether this is true or not, Schwinn did bring the average customer from a 3-speed to a 10-speed model with little alteration in his cycling position. Although this may not seem like a great feat the prevalent attitude that the "bent over" position was uncomfortable had to be changed, as well as the image of the bicycle as a toy. Once adults began riding their new 10-speeds, they realized that the "bent over" position was actually comfortable and more efficient than the upright position.

Arnold, Schwinn & Company was incorporated in 1895 by Adolph Arnold and Ignaz Schwinn. They were interested in manufacturing and selling bicycles and their parts. Arnold, Schwinn & Company was the brainchild of Ignaz Schwinn who had come to this country in 1891 and had become frustrated working for other bicycle companies. His whole life showed initiative and genius that had been unfulfilled working for others.

Ignaz Schwinn was born in 1860 in Baden, Germany. At a very early age, he became a machinist's apprentice and began working on the "invention of the age," the bicycle. Ignaz went from factory to factory trying to find a niche for himself. Frustrated, he began designing bicycles on his own while working at various machine shops. His design of an improved *safety* bicycle interested Heinrich Kleyer, a small builder of high-wheeled bicycles. Subsequently, Kleyer hired Ignaz Schwinn as a designer and factory manager. The Kleyer factory started producing some of the first safety bicycles in Germany. Although the Kleyer factory prospered, Ignaz Schwinn was still not satisfied.

Background

When he was 31, Ignaz Schwinn emigrated to Chicago. In Chicago, as in Germany, Ignaz worked in a number of factories designing bicycles. But Schwinn was not content; he wanted to build bikes for himself. By 1894 Ignaz Schwinn had met Adolph Arnold who was the president of Arnold Brothers, a meat-packing establishment, and president of the Haymarket Produce Bank. Adolph Arnold had faith in the genius of Ignaz and provided him with the financial backing necessary to start a bicycle factory.

A building was rented on the corner of Lake and Peoria streets. Ignaz Schwinn designed the bicycles and the tools to make them, purchased the machinery and equipment, and hired the personnel needed to operate the factory. Schwinn began operation of his factory in 1895 at the height of the bicycle boom. When he started production, there were probably 300 other bicycle factories and as many assembly shops already operating in the United States. In spite of the many manufacturers, nobody was able to produce enough bicycles to satisfy demand. However, like most trends, the bicycle boom died by 1899 and most of the bicycle manufacturers closed their doors. The bicycle racing stars of the 1890s, who were some of the best riders in the world, quickly faded, leaving their European counterparts the task of developing racing bicycles and equipment. As the United States slipped into the middle ages in bicycle activity, Europe experienced its renaissance.

Although Ignaz Schwinn had to cut back on production, his sound management and good product line allowed him to remain profitable. In 1908 Ignaz Schwinn bought out his partner Adolph Arnold and thus became the sole owner of Arnold, Schwinn & Co. The name remained unchanged until 1967 when it became the Schwinn Bicycle Company.

Unlike many bicycle manufacturers, Schwinn has always

been interested in further expanding its markets. But to educate an apathetic U.S. population in the 1920s was no easy task! Schwinn started a full-scale marketing campaign to encourage the sale and use of bicycles. Historians might well claim that Schwinn brought the American bicycle business out of the depression and into a recovery period by introducing *balloon* tires, *front-wheel expander brakes* operated by a hand lever on the handlebars, a *drop-forged handlebar stem*, a full-floating saddle and seatpost, knee-action spring fork, and other design features.

Schwinn's eagerness to promote bicycling activities began in the 1890s with the support of a racing team known as the world team, which exposed thousands of fans to the excitement of racing. When the track at Garfield Park in Chicago opened on October 3, 1896, twenty-five thousand people watched Jimmy Michael, a star rider for the world team, break the American five-mile record!

Another spurt of enthusiasm came in the 1930s when six-day racing, which originated in Madison Square Garden during the depression, became popular. At the time, most riders were using European-built bicycles and components because the previous decline in bicycle sales had forced all the American companies to cut back production. There were, however, a few small custom builders in this country such as Wastyn and Drysdale who were still building racing bicycles.

Emil Wastyn had a small frame-building shop in Chicago, located not far from the Schwinn factory. Ignaz Schwinn, being eager to promote cycling, hired Emil Wastyn on a consulting basis to help him design a quality American bicycle suitable for six-day racing. The result was the Paramount track bicycle built with Accles and Pollack (an English tubing company) double-butted tubing, English cast lugs, and specially designed and built Schwinn hubs and cranks. As soon as the Paramount track bicycle went on the market, American riders demanded the bike.

To help promote cycling, Ignaz Schwinn again sponsored a racing team. This time, the team was called the Schwinn Paramount racing team. Some of the best six-day riders in the United States, including Jerry Rodman and Jimmy Walthour were on the Schwinn team. Although there was much enthusiasm for six-day races in the 1930s, this enthusiasm waned with the onset of World War II and never recovered. After the war, Americans were too busy buying refrigerators, washing machines, and automobiles to pay much attention to bicycles and bicycle racing.

The most recent demonstration of Schwinn's continued support for bicycle racing came in 1974 when the Amateur Bicycle League (now the United States Cycling Federation), the governing body of amateur U.S. cycling at the time, allowed sponsorship of amateur riders. Schwinn presently provides sponsorship for five different amateur racing clubs across the country, one of which is the Wolverines (now called the Wolverine–Schwinn Sports Club) which has provided Schwinn with champions such as Sheila Young, Sue Novara, and Roger Young, all of whom ride Schwinn Paramounts. (Before the sponsorship, Sheila Young rode a Cinelli track bicycle and Sue Novara rode a Pogliaghi.)

Building Philosophy

When Schwinn began building its standard-line Paramount bicycles in the 1950s, Nervex lugs were used. Twenty years later, Schwinn is still building the Paramounts with Nervex lugs. In the 1950s, the Nervex lug was the most popular design as well as a quality product. Today, the fashion is the smooth, simple Italian-type lug. As a result, Schwinn has been seriously thinking about changing. Like other changes that Schwinn makes, however, it has to be carefully researched and developed. Schwinn is interested in more than the overall finish of the lug. They are primarily concerned with accuracy of internal diameters, maintenance of the angles, and the quality of the threading and facing of the bottom brackets.

Schwinn used cast lugs in the 1930s when the first six-day frames were made but the lugs were sand castings, which resulted in rough, pitted finishes. The casting process has been greatly improved since then and Schwinn is presently looking at some investment cast lugs, bottom brackets, and fork crowns only because the castings are able to achieve fine definition that requires less hand finishing.

Various fork crowns are used on the Paramounts: on the road, a pressed steel Nervex crown; on the track, a forged Japanese crown; and on the tandem, a specially machined crown out of a solid block of steel. Although Schwinn is considering using cast fork crowns on the Paramounts, they believe that it is not necessary since the weakest part of the fork is the blades. If engineering were the only consideration, Brilando would probably use a heavier-gauge fork blade than a cast fork since he believes "an ideally designed fork should give uniformly throughout."

Most of the forks that Schwinn uses are preraked at Reynolds to Schwinn's specifications. Schwinn furnishes Reynolds with a drawing indicating the exact dimensions needed. The fork rakes currently used are:

1. 1⅜ inches on the track frames;
2. 1¾ inches on the road frames;
3. 1½ inches on the criterium frames.

Interestingly, 1¾-inch fork rakes are used on both the touring and the road racing models. Until recently, the touring bicycles used a 2-inch fork rake but laboratory tests confirmed that ¼ inch less gave the tourist a more stable and safer ride.

Schwinn was probably one of the first builders to use the large ⅝-inch stays on their standard frames. According to Brilando, with ⅝-inch seatstays "you can get greater lightness as well as stiffness by using a lighter-gauge tube."

The Paramounts incorporate a seatstay attachment that is chamfered with small pieces of metal used to cap the seatstays. Other seatstay clusters have been considered but all were rejected on the belief that there is no advantage of adding extra weight in this area by using top eyes or wraparounds, which require heavy fixtures to give their neat appearance. Schwinn's analysis found that some of the so-called lightweight fastback stays use a heavy piece of metal built into the lug to allow an adequate brazing surface. As Frank Brilando sees it, "People try and save weight in the tubing and they add weight on the seat lug! That doesn't make sense. I would rather see that weight put into the tubing to give you overall frame stiffness than something just for cosmetics."

All Paramounts (road, track, tandem, custom) are built on jigs. There are only two brazers, Lucille and Wanda, who work on the Paramounts. They are probably the only women in the industry who braze top-quality frames! Lucille and Wanda have been brazing Paramounts for more than 25 years and they do an extraordinary job using a small flame and the lowest possible temperature. They have learned to control the torch to keep the tubes as cool as possible during the brazing process to maintain

Figure 17-1: Ferenc Makos, at an aligning table, makes sure the Paramount frame is perfectly aligned and straight.

the tube's physical properties. Silver solder is used for braze primarily to minimize overheating the tubing. With the lower temperature required to braze with the silver, it is possible to rigidly hold the frame in a jig and expect minimal distortion in the frame. "If a braze with a higher melting point was used and everything was jigged and held rigidly, there would be no room for expansion of parts," Brilando claims. "With our system of jigging and use of silver solder, we keep everything very much in line.'' The entire frame is silver-soldered except the dropouts. On these, brass is used because the fits are not as good; there is generally more than .003 inch of space that has to be filled.

The tandems present another problem. They are also built in rigidly held jigs, but they are bronze-welded (fillet-brazed) because they do not have lugs. Of course, there would be much distortion if the tubing were lightweight but with the use of

Figure 17-2: Schwinn is the only company we visited that exclusively uses women to handle all brazing. Here Lucille Redman works on a Paramount frame as she has done for around 30 years.

heavier straight gauge tubing, the expansion and contraction of the tubing is minimized.

Working together with the two brazers are two other frame builders who perform the actual assembling of frames. They work from specifications; cut, miter, and flux all the tubes; and accurately assemble the entire frame in the jig. After the setup is complete, the frame is brazed by either Lucille or Wanda. The majority of the tubes for the standard Paramounts are mitered on a special milling lathe. However, on the custom frames, the majority are hand-mitered because it is faster and easier to hand-miter than it is to reset the lathe.

If any one aspect of the building process was singled out as the most important, Frank Brilando believes he would have to choose the brazing process.

The brazing is more important than the mitering. Still, I don't know how you can separate them. You can have a poorly mitered tube and a good braze job and nobody would know the difference provided you've got a rigid lug because the body of the lug is so much greater than the tube that you'll never see. Any failures will always go beyond the lug on the tube. If you have a good sturdy lug, the fitting of the tubes isn't going to be that critical. I think that a lot is overemphasized because the joint of the tube is so minimal compared to the strength of a lug. If you have very thin lugs, then I would say that the mitering becomes very important.

Frank believes that unless someone has a lot of experience brazing, it is easy to be fooled into thinking that you have a good joint, because it is difficult to know whether the braze has gone all the way into the joint. There are many things that Frank believes are important: proper preparation of the joint, cleaning it properly, fitting up the joint, getting the right heat to sweat-in the braze; but these are all things that you cannot see by looking at the frame. *Consequently, the reputation of the builder becomes the primary guide to whether you have a good frame or not.*

After the frames are built, they are checked for alignment. Even with the careful precision with which Schwinn builds its

Paramounts, there can be a small amount of warpage that occurs in the hangar bracket. In order to realign the frame, the bottom bracket is retapped. The outer face of the bottom bracket is then faced off, after which a precision *cone and locknut* is screwed into the bottom bracket. This cone and locknut fits on a fixed mandrel on a precision aligning table. The frame is aligned (cold set) to the threads themselves in the bottom bracket.

Schwinn uses a process similar to sandblasting, called *glass beading,* to clean the frame and prepare it for painting. It resembles sandblasting except that it uses a much finer material which is less likely to score the frame. The Paramount frames are painted with the standard Schwinn paint used on the other Schwinn production frames. The only difference is that the Paramounts are all hand-sprayed whereas the production frames are done electrostatically. The translucent finishes receive a primer, silver, and final coat. The opaque finishes receive only a primer and topcoat.

When a custom order is received, it is sent to the product design area where Charles "Spike" Shannon, Paramount designer, reviews it and lays out the dimensions on the drafting board to make sure that there are no design problems. If there is a problem, Spike will work with the customer, resolving any difficulties. There have been times, of course, when he has been unable to convince the customer and has refused an order because he thought it was unsound. Schwinn has the ability to give the customer exactly what he wants. The wait for a custom order can vary from one to four months depending on the time of year. Custom tandem orders do not take any longer since all custom orders go right into rotation as they are received.

Schwinn's Paramount production is very small. Out of one million Schwinn frames that are built each year, only 800 are Paramounts. The majority of Schwinns manufactured are the lugless, flash-welded models (which, in fact, are not lugless at all, because they have a head lug and bottom bracket lug that are flash-welded together). As required by the flash-welding process, heavier-walled welded tubing is used. Consequently, these bicycles are durable but heavy.

A number of Schwinn models have also been built in Japan to Schwinn's specifications. These bicycles have been the production lugged frame models which Schwinn was not equipped to produce when their popularity skyrocketed with the bicycle boom in 1973. Since that time, Schwinn has been working on setting up production for lugged frames. Soon, Schwinn will be producing production-line lugged frames in its factory in Chicago. This will mean that once again all Schwinn bicycles will be made in the United States.

Figure 17-3: Charles Shannon, engineer, checking wheel clearance on a custom bicycle design.

Frame Selection

During the 1950s, Schwinn started building road racing Paramounts and, like the track bicycles, they were only built on a custom basis. Schwinn miscalculated the popularity of the Paramounts because when the demand increased in the 1950s, Schwinn was not equipped to handle it and had to hire Oscar Wastyn, Sr., to help build some of the Paramounts. Oscar learned how to build bicycles from his father (Emil) and took over his father's small bicycle store and frame-building shop which is still located near the Schwinn factory today. Now the store is operated by the third generation of cycling Wastyns, Oscar Wastyn, Jr.

With the many custom orders Schwinn was getting for the road Paramount, it was time to incorporate the Paramount into the standard Schwinn line. By 1956, all the bicycles supplied to the U.S. Olympic Cycling Team were built by Schwinn using Reynolds 531DB tubing and Campagnolo equipment. (Schwinn had used Accles and Pollack tubing before World War II, but it was not available in the 1950s.) Schwinn had conducted years of research and testing and by 1956 concluded that the best racing materials were made by TI Reynolds and Campagnolo. To this day, most of the Paramounts are still being built with Reynolds 531DB tubing and equipped with Campagnolo components.

In 1958, the Paramount road bicycle became a standard model in the Schwinn line. The standard Paramount was designed to fit the size requirements of 99 percent of the population. For riders with specific requirements, Schwinn has continued to build custom Paramounts for road or track use.

When the Paramount road-racing model first became part of the Schwinn standard line, it did not reflect the designs of the ordinary racing bicycle. Schwinn was one of the first builders to use steep angles on road bicycles. (In the 1950s, all road bicycles had much shallower angles.) Schwinn believed that since the American roads were so smooth, a road bicycle should be designed more along track lines for better, more responsive handling.

Frank Brilando, vice-president in charge of engineering, has been with Schwinn since 1951. His credentials are extensive, including a berth on the 1948 and 1952 U.S. Olympic teams. He believes that Schwinn can satisfy almost every taste and need. If

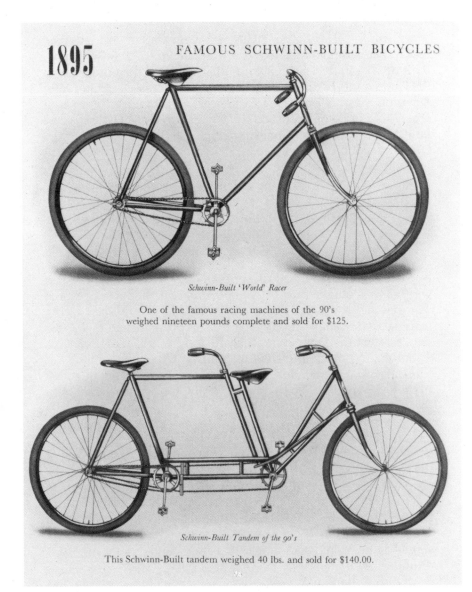

1895 FAMOUS SCHWINN-BUILT BICYCLES

Schwinn-Built 'World' Racer

One of the famous racing machines of the 90's
weighed nineteen pounds complete and sold for $125.

Schwinn-Built Tandem of the 90's

This Schwinn-Built tandem weighed 40 lbs. and sold for $140.00.

Figure 17-4: The relatively small degree of change in bicycle frame design becomes immediately obvious when we compare yesterday's bicycles with today's.

OF YESTERDAY AND TODAY

1945

Schwinn-Built 'Paramount' Racer

Up to World War II, the 'Paramount' was the only all-American Racer used in the six-day races.

A Modern Schwinn-Built Tandem

The ultra modern deluxe version of 'The Bicycle Built for Two'

the needs are not met in the standard line, a special custom design can be provided.

Like Cinelli, Schwinn's building and design philosophy stresses rigidity over extreme lightness. For example, since it is difficult to build a good, stiff frame in a large size, Schwinn uses heavier-gauge tubing to achieve stiffness as the size of the frame increases. Extra-heavy chainstays and fork blades are used on all models. On extremely large frames (in excess of 26 inches), straight gauge SAE 4130 chrome molybdenum is used for the down tube and the seat tube. By combining this tubing with a stiffer front fork, Schwinn has been able to overcome a lot of the tracking problems that occur on large frames when riding down-hill and riding without hands. Through years of experience Schwinn has opted for rigidity rather than lightness.

Frank Brilando doesn't believe that there's a great difference between the chrome molybdenum tubing and the Reynolds manganese-molybdenum tubing as far as the end product is concerned. He does believe that a little more caution has to be used when working with chrome molybdenum tubings because overheating and rapid cooling will cause more brittleness in the frame joints than with manganese molybdenum. Why does Schwinn use chrome molybdenum tubing more extensively? According to Brilando, "We've found the Reynolds tubing to be very good and there's no reason to change just for the sake of changing. Furthermore, 531 has good acceptance by the public."

Frank Brilando believes that you cannot consider the top tube dimensions by themselves since they are influenced by the other frame specifications. As a rule, top tube length should not be a controlling factor in ordering a custom frame because if, for example, a shallow seat angle is requested (and everything else is constant) a longer top tube will be required. "Top tube length by itself doesn't mean an awful lot unless you tie it into the complete bicycle."

Schwinn is probably the only large manufacturer in the world that makes a top-line touring model. The design of Schwinn's standard line touring model has been tested and retested to insure a safe and comfortable ride. The touring Paramount has a slightly longer wheelbase, due to a longer rear triangle, which distributes the weight of the rider and the touring load more evenly on the frame. Through testing, Schwinn has found that a slightly longer rear end (⅜ inch) will transfer some of the weight to the front of the bicycle and the better weight distribution will contribute greatly to the safety of the rider. If you know that the ⅜-inch longer stay gives you better weight distribution, what would happen if the rear triangle were lengthened by an additional ⅝ inch? Schwinn's tests have shown that a longer rear triangle will create instability and make the bicycle handling unwieldy. The ⅜-inch longer stay that Schwinn uses is the best compromise.

One of the greatest problems a tourist has to face is riding downhill with the weight of touring packs on the bicycle. Again, Schwinn has performed tests which indicate that the racer shares the problem of instability on downhills, but that his problem is more manageable because he is riding without bulky packs. The downhill problem is exacerbated when carriers and packs are attached to the bicycle, especially, as Brilando notes, "when rear carriers are not anchored solidly. They tend to shimmy and this transfers through the whole bicycle."

To help eliminate this dangerous situation, Schwinn's testing has confirmed that:

1. carriers must be solidly secured to the frame;
2. carriers must be strong enough to support the packs;
3. the packs must securely fasten to the carrier, to insure as little movement as possible;
4. the weight should be distributed in the panniers with the heavy items at the bottom.

If you are going to use front panniers, the same criteria apply. Of course, overloading front panniers will cause a dangerously unstable condition. Although most people seem to be using front handlebar packs, Schwinn has not done any conclusive testing in this area, but Brilando believes "if it is rigidly held, it is not too bad. If it slops around, then you get into instability problems."

The road racing Paramount that Schwinn offers in its standard line is designed for long-distance road races. A special lighter criterium frame is offered but only as a custom order. The same applies to the track frame. The standard Paramount track frame is built for sprints while lighter pursuit frames can be ordered on a custom basis. Although Schwinn uses Reynolds 531DB on all its frames, the tube gauges are heavier than the standard-packaged Reynolds 531DB sets. The reason for the heavier tubing is the belief that frame rigidity is affected more by the tubing than by the lug. Since frame rigidity is the basis of Schwinn's design philosophy, the necessity for thicker-gauge tubing becomes essential. According to Brilando, "Lightness is great for certain specific applications but generally for most usage, we tend toward the stiff side. We have built extra-light bicycles for pursuit and time trialing and so forth, but you have to apply the bicycle to the type of usage."

On the standard track, road racing, and road touring Paramounts, the top tube is 18/21 gauge, the down tube 19/22, the seat tube 21/24, the chainstays are 18/20, and the fork blades 17/20. When building special pursuit and criterium frames, special lightweight tubing is used, producing frames 1½ to 2 pounds lighter than standard frames. Although lighter Reynolds tubing is used on many of the custom bicycles, Schwinn does use Columbus and Ishiwata tubing as well. The Ishiwata tubing is called for when light specialty frames are required.

Like most respected master builders, Schwinn takes a conservative approach to frame building, emphasizing strength over lightness. Although the Paramount lacks some of the glamour and mystique of the foreign bicycles, it is superbly built and priced competitively. Most important, the generous warranty provides *free* frame repairs if a failure is due to faulty materials or workmanship.

CHAPTER 18
Profiles of Some American Frame Builders

F. M. Assenmacher
   Lightweight Cycles
104 East May Street
Mount Pleasant, MI 48858

Matt Assenmacher is a builder from the "traditional school." Looking into his background, it is easy to see why. He learned to build bikes while he served as an apprentice for a year at JRJ Cycles, Limited, in England (see chapter 5).

The majority of the American builders use Du Pont's Imron paint because of its resistance to chipping. The British, on the other hand, increase the chip resistance of their paints by their methods of applying the paint. While Imron is fairly easy to apply and it requires a minimum of steps, the British processes require several steps. Accordingly, the actual painting of the frames has become a British trademark.

It comes as no surprise that Matt's bicycles have a very British look. He learned the basics from Bob Jackson. Matt's paint process is involved and can best be described in his own words:

> Painting is a six-step process beginning with the removal of all oxides from the bare frame by a light sandblasting. The bare frame is then chemically treated with rust-inhibiting bonding agents which eliminate rust problems and also bond the paint film to the metal. The frame is then primed and enamelled with Sherwin-Williams professional paint system. The transfers and the hand lining are done at this time. After the transfers have cured, the frame is finished with a special two-part clear acrylic for added durability and gloss. The paint then cures in about 24 hours and the frame is ready for assembly.

Under the paint job, Assenmacher's frames are orthodox in design and construction. Like the Europeans, Matt does not use a jig for brazing the main triangle. Only the forks and rearstays are brazed in a jig. All Assenmacher frames are silver-brazed and are built personally by Matt. His one assistant handles only the cleanup, sandblasting, and initial paint preparation steps. The decision of which gauge and type of tubing to be used is made after Matt learns the size and weight of the rider, his or her riding style, the ultimate use of the frame, and the rider's individual preferences.

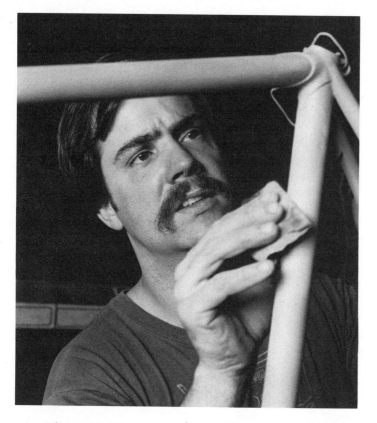

Figure 18-1: Assenmacher putting the finishing touches on one of his frames.

Assenmacher, who has been building frames since 1973, currently builds about two a week. In addition to his custom frame building, he has a constant supply of frame repairs for other competitive brands. His frame repair business is strong because people have learned of his quality workmanship. Furthermore, there are proportionately fewer frame builders in the Midwest than in the West.

Assenmacher is eager to please his customers and he will build racing or touring bicycles and tandems. He is particularly cognizant of the needs of the tourist and will supply brazed-on frame fittings in any configuration desired by the customer. Although he is only 27 years old, he has been an enthusiastic cyclist for over half of his life. Currently he is succeeding in providing the kind of service that is difficult to duplicate when dealing overseas, while at the same time, is building a bicycle that compares favorably with those built by the British.

Bill Boston
38 Franklin Street
PO Box 114
Swedesboro, NJ 08085

It is difficult to find a "unique" American frame builder since, in general, all share an important similarity—they specialize in building individual bikes for individual customers. You could examine their complete production for a year without finding two identical frames. Like his compeititors, Bill Boston specializes in matching the individual needs of a rider. He has taken the art of properly sizing the frame one step further, however. He has constructed an "adjustable" frameset with variable seat angles, top tube height, bottom bracket height, and top tube lengths. After personally determining the basic parameters of the "ideal" frame with the customer astride the adjustable frame, Bill attempts to determine the individual needs of the customer—a racing or touring frame, for instance.

Like many of the popular builders, Bill Boston is young. He's in his early thirties. He started building frames, on a part-time basis, in 1972. By 1975, the demand for his products reached the point where he decided to make bicycle frame building his sole livelihood.

After high school, Bill worked for a short time at Du Pont and then joined the navy. For six months of his navy experience he built jet engines. Because of his desire to "learn more about those jet engines than anyone in the shop" he quickly became quality control inspector. After the navy, Bill rejoined the work force at Du Pont and his interest in cycling began.

Bill's introduction to cycling came through his brother who was an avid rider. Bill's real commitment began when he restored a 1937 Drysdale track bike, his first real bike. In many ways, the Drysdale was a major contributor in Bill's decision to manufacture bicycles. The fine construction of the old bicycle was immediately obvious to Bill as he compared it to some of the alleged high-quality modern frames. Bill flew to England to meet with Reynolds and discuss his individual tubing requirements. He also visited several of the well-known British builders to pick up

Figure 18-2: Bill Boston's frame fitting jig. Note precise fitting in detail photograph (figure 18-3).

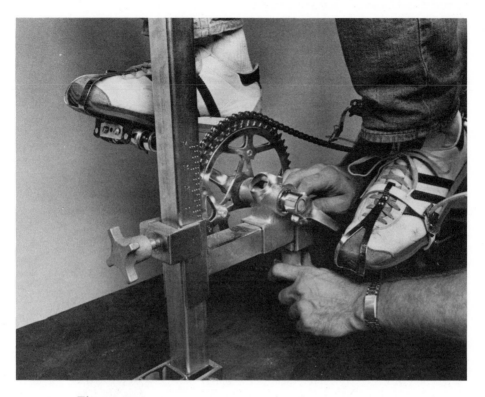

Figure 18-3

pointers. His strong technical background left him disenchanted with the British builders and their reliance on what Bill felt was "feel" rather than technology.

Although Bill Boston's annual production is only approximately 50 frames, or less if there is a high proportion of tandems, the number is not a true indication of his potential. Much of his time is devoted to his hand-manufacture of special handlebar stems (each one takes 12 to 14 hours to produce), integral allen key seat tube fittings, and custom racks for touring. Bill likes to think of himself as a craftsman and his concern for the quality of his products is greater than the profit associated with the venture.

Initially, all Bill Boston frames were jig-built with brass, but he has since switched to silver. The switch was made after Bill had learned to properly match the bicycle tubes with their lugs, which required, in Bill's words, "remanufacturing the lugs." Although the cost of silver greatly exceeds that of brass, the extra cost is made up in the reduced time required to file and clean the joints when using silver.

According to Bill, it took him over a year to complete his bicycle design theories. Some of his answers were developed on a computer which he used to determine frame stress. Apparently, Bill did his homework well since he appears to be very knowledgeable about the relationship between frame design and the physical capabilities of a rider. Boston makes no bones about the relationship of the seat angle and the rider's pedaling techniques, "if they like to spin they get a steep seat angle. If they don't like to spin and they like to push hard, they get a shallow seat angle." In our travels, we found builders generally had a better understanding of the technical requirements of brazing than knowledge of the mechanics of riding. Boston was an exception.

Bill Boston prides himself on solving the needs of the serious cyclist and he has many methods of building frames for the very short or very tall person. He will not build a frame to meet an individual's specifications unless he feels that the design is sound. Although Bill does build racing bicycles, his forte is touring bicycles. He finds that he has many more touring cyclists for customers than he does racers. Consequently, he has studied and tested his touring designs more frequently.

Francisco Cuevas of
Paris Sport Cycle
186 Main Street
Ridgefield Park, NJ 07660

Few craftsmen have been building frames longer than Francisco Cuevas*. In his forty-third year of frame building he is still brazing and designing frames with the same enthusiasm and determination that characterized his idealistic youth. The great frame builders seem to be inexorably drawn by the hope their next frame will be the "perfect frame." Similarly, Cuevas builds each frame as if it were a work of art to be admired and enjoyed.

Francisco Cuevas also has the distinction of having built frames on three different continents. He started building frames in

---

*As the book went to press, we learned that Cuevas had left Paris Sport Cycle.

1925 when he worked for a factory in his hometown of Barcelona, Spain. In 1928 he started his apprenticeship under two Spanish frame builders, Ernesto Bayo and Jose Magdalena. By 1932 Cuevas was confident of his ability as a frame builder and he opened his own frame-building shop in Barcelona. His success was not immediate, however. His competitors claimed that he was too inexperienced to be proficient. His products proved otherwise. Through hard work and discipline the talented Cuevas quickly established himself as one of the major frame builders in Barcelona.

In the 1930s Spain was a time bomb of political unrest. The political factions exploded into a full-scale civil war and Cuevas found that the emotionalism of the time led him to join the Loyalist forces. Forsaking his shop, he began a life pledged to establishing a stable democratic rule in Spain. When Franco's

Figure 18-4: Cuevas with apprentice.

army firmly established itself as the ruling authority, Cuevas fled across the border to France where he spent eight months in a refugee camp.

By late 1941 the political situation had normalized and Cuevas returned to Spain. He reopened his shop and again began building frames. Once again his shop prospered, but the situation in Spain continued to deteriorate.

In 1951, unable to tolerate the political regime, Cuevas left for Argentina. He spent 18 years in Argentina as a successful frame builder where his firm, Ciclos Cuevas, employed four assistants. He developed a close association with the bicycle federation and became the technical director of the Mendoza district bicycle federation. Unfortunately, the political situation in Argentina in the 1960s was highly explosive and again Cuevas felt that he had to leave. He emigrated to the United States in 1969.

Cuevas' individual success in the United States has been marginal. Without the capital investment needed to establish another shop, he was forced to work as a bicycle technician and consultant in many of the larger bicycle stores in the New York City area.

Since 1976, Francisco Cuevas has firmly established himself with Paris Sport Cycle which provides him with a frame-building workshop. Although the frames he builds all bear the Paris Sport label, they can be distinguished from Paris Sports' "other" master builder, Pepi Limongi, by the signature on the rear chainstay of the frame.

Cuevas is a builder from the "old school" of frame building who believes that it is imperative to learn how to handle a file properly before even looking at a torch. According to Cuevas, learning how to handle a file requires years of careful filing and finishing frames.

Cuevas welds with either silver or brass. Since he is so familiar with the effects of heat on lightweight bicycle tubing, he feels that the normal objection to brass (increased possibility of overheating the tubes) doesn't exist in his case.

All the tubes are spot-tacked to insure correct alignment of all frame dimensions. Cuevas does not use frame jigs because he feels that the expansion that takes place when heating the tubes must take place unhindered, otherwise the frame will distort upon cooling, requiring much more bending when cold setting the

Figure 18-5: Nearly 50 years of experience guide the hands of craftsman Cuevas as he files the fork crown tangs.

frame. With his years of experience he finds that he can second-guess the reaction of the tubing, thus eliminating the need for extensive cold setting.

Mike Fraysse, owner of Paris Sport Cycle, advised us that Cuevas will build almost any frame size imaginable—from 18-inch racing frames to 28-inch touring frames. The large-size frames he designs handle well, according to Mike, but in the European tradition, he would rather see a tall person ride a frame that is as small as possible because a smaller frame will naturally handle better.

THE CUSTOM BICYCLE

Albert Eisentraut
1000 Twenty-second Avenue
Oakland, CA 94606

Albert Eisentraut is probably the most famous of the current American frame builders. The story behind Eisentraut is especially interesting because it is a real-life example of what often happens when a small, high-quality frame builder tries to meet his demand by increasing the number of employees and semi-mass producing frames. Because of poor capitalization, quality control, and labor problems, Eisentraut has abandoned the project, reverting back to the production style that made him famous: He once again builds all of the frames himself. Before we look at Albert's current frame-building operation, let's look at the events that contributed to the man and his bicycles.

Since he grew up in a cycling family, Albert Eisentraut's experience more closely parallels that of the European frame builder than any of his American counterparts. Albert's father was a prominent bicycle racer who actively competed in the 1930s. His close friend was Oscar Wastyn, Sr., the well-respected frame builder and bike shop owner. From the age of three, Albert visited the shop regularly with his father, and in 1955, at the age of 15, began working for Oscar as a bicycle mechanic. Oscar liked Albert and would spend hours talking and philosophizing with him on the merits of cycling. At the same time, Albert's father, an adept welder by profession, taught his son how to braze. Both Oscar and his father became major influences in his life.

Albert's technical skills continued to improve while he attended the Illinois Institute of Technology's program for mechanical engineering. In addition to his formal education during the day, Albert worked part time in an ironworks where he became more familiar with machine tool operation. He built a few experimental frames at that time, although "they were recreational frames for my own amusement." Throughout this time his interest in bicycle racing continued to grow and when he joined the army in 1961, he was at his racing peak.

The army recognized Albert's racing experience (a second-place finish in the Illinois state championships, a tenth-place finish at the national championships, and numerous individual race victories) and placed him as one of the members of its cycling team. The army stationed Albert in Oakland, California, and, after his stint with the army, he entered San Jose State College. Four years after leaving the army and a curriculum change later, Albert received a B.A. in art. Two years later, in 1967, Albert received a teaching certificate and an M.A. in ceramic sculpture. As an undergraduate Albert worked part-time as a bicycle mechanic and continued to experiment in frame building. Even when he was a full-time graduate student and teaching assistant in art, he continued to work on various aspects of frame building. In 1969, after teaching for two years, Albert decided to devote his full attention to frame building.

The Eisentraut frame has gained strong popularity among American racers. This is particularly unique since most of the production of the American builders is usually touring bicycles.

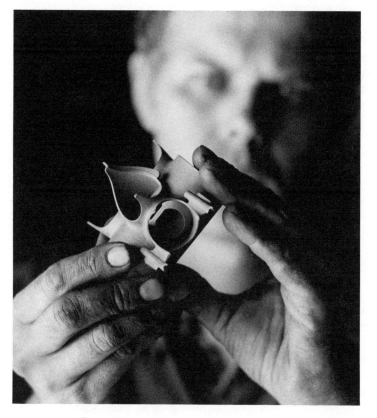

Figure 18-6: Eisentraut examines a custom lug.

The top American bicycle racers ride the prestigious European frames. Of the many American bicycles, only the Eisentrauts and the Schwinn Paramounts have gained wide racing appeal. How did Eisentraut earn his reputation?

Albert is a major influence in modern American cycling partially as a result of his successful synthesis of his many years of experience. Although he is only 38, he had been producing custom-made bicycles years before the bicycle boom. Maximizing the benefits of his racing experience, his technical skills, and his artistic talents, Albert was able to design and produce a frame that was aesthetically pleasing and technically sound. He could offer his customers more than just a well-brazed bicycle; he could interpret their physical requirements into an efficient frame design. In response to the great demand for his frames, Albert chose to meet that demand with a semi-mass produced frame called the "Limited."

By semi-mass producing the Limited, Albert was able to meet his demand with a less-expensive Eisentraut frame. But, because of the lack of capital investment needed to adequately mechanize many of the frame-building procedures and the shortage of qualified labor and its attendant quality control problems, Albert abandoned the project. He found that he sometimes produced a substandard Eisentraut frame, not the quality product with a reasonable price tag as he had envisioned at the commencement of the project. As Albert described his problems, it sounded reminiscent of complaints voiced by other famous builders in Europe. Albert found that "Unskilled people . . . don't particularly care and they don't think that it's (the assembly process) particularly important and the kind of work they turn out is definitely substandard. The more skilled people very quickly tire and want to make more money." But where does this money come from? Virtually every builder we spoke with is motivated by the desire to create a quality product—not by the desire to turn a large profit. As a result of Albert's unsatisfactory experience with the Limited, he has decided to return to being a one-man operation that exclusively specializes in custom frames.

Albert builds all of his frames on jigs. The tubes are mitered on a lathe and the frames may be brass- or silver-brazed depending usually on the gauge of the tubing being used. For Albert, the gauge of the tubing is very important and he selects his tubes according to the design requirement of each frame and not according to what an individual tubing company offers. Consequently, a single Eisentraut frame may be built with more than one kind of tubing, whether it is Columbus, Reynolds, Ishiwata, Tanguy, or Super Vitus.

The frame jigs which Albert uses are interesting because he has designed them to allow for expansion of the tubing during the brazing process. This reduces the tendency of the frame to have inbuilt stresses. Once the frame has been built and cleaned, it is finished with Du Pont Imron paint, a standard practice among many of the quality American builders.

Through the years Albert has kept all of the sizes of his customers and the dimensions of their respective frames. He uses this information to assist in sizing each new customer. He also uses an interesting variation on determining the length of the seat tube. To calculate the length of the seat tube, he requires a rider to be measured while laying on the floor with the balls of his or her feet against the wall. This will usually result in the foot extending toward the wall at approximately a 45-degree angle. With Albert's method, the inseam measurement to the wall will include the effect of foot size.

Recently, Albert has developed investment cast lugs which are relatively lightweight and are more accurate than the normal pressed lug. He has no intentions of producing them commercially, however.

The bicycle purist should be happy to know that the United States' strongest candidate for the title of master builder has returned to personally producing all Albert Eisentraut frames and that once again we can buy a frame with the quality that made the name famous.

Bruce Gordon Cycles
27729 Clear Lake Road
Eugene, OR 97402

Unlike many American frame builders, Bruce Gordon seems to have a very businesslike view of frame building. While some are artisans who do not care to be bothered with the day-to-day problems inherent in a business, Bruce tends to be a careful technician who is as skilled at talking about frames as he is competent in building them.

Although Bruce is just barely 30 years old, he has a varied

cycling background. He was employed as a bicycle mechanic for two years and then became a manager. After three years of store management, he found that he longed for work that required making expressive use of his hands. In 1974 he started working as an apprentice for the frame builder Albert Eisentraut. Soon he became a part owner in the newly reorganized corporation. But like many partnerships, the owners sometimes had trouble agreeing on the direction and philosophy of the company. In 1976 Bruce sold his share of the business to Eisentraut and moved to Oregon to start his own frame-building operation.

Bruce Gordon is a perfectionist and he believes that it is virtually impossible to produce near-perfect frames without the finest machinery available. His annual production of 100 to 125 frames per year is the result of his large capital investment in machine tools and his organized business sense. Every sequence in the frame-building operation is done with the most sophisticated equipment appropriate to the particular job to be performed. Tubes are mitered precisely with a milling machine. Several custom-made jigs are employed for each step of the frame-brazing process.

Bruce has his own sandblasting booth. He believes the booth is necessary to properly clean the tubes and lugs before and after the brazing process. Although he has the paint work performed by someone else, he is in the process of setting up an area to do his own. Like many American builders, Bruce uses only Du Pont Imron paint.

During our interviews of frame builders we found that few really understood the business fundamentals necessary to operate a successful business. Accordingly, a surprisingly large number of American builders went "out of business" during the preparation of this book. Bruce, on the other hand, recognizes that his large investment in machinery may never reach the levels of return expected by the average investor. He believes that the equipment is required, however, to produce a truly top-quality frame. He is the first builder that we spoke to who shares our belief that some builders are required to charge high prices since they haven't spent time researching how to perform each required step in the frame-building process on an efficient, as well as, high-quality basis.

Technically, Bruce Gordon is conservative compared to other young American builders. He silver-brazes with Reynolds or

Columbus tubing and doesn't believe there is any great difference between the two brands of tubing. He believes that matching the gauge of the tubing to the ultimate use of the bicycle is more important than what brand of tubing is used. His bicycles are built with Cinelli or Prugnat lugs and they usually include the Cinelli semi-sloping crown and investment cast bottom bracket. His fastback stays are his "trademark" and are built with a normal seat lug that has had the "ears" removed and a plate welded over the gap.

When we asked Bruce his opinions on how long it takes to become a skilled frame builder, his answer was unique. He believes that the easiest part of the frame-building operation, the

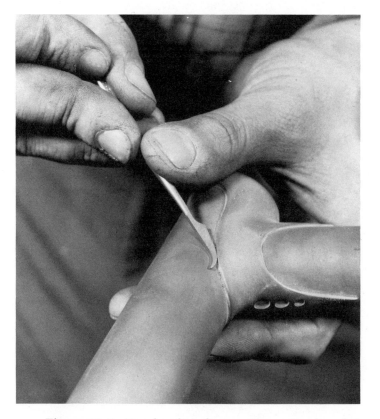

Figure 18-7: Hands of craftsman Bruce Gordon doing finishing work around the lug.

paint finish, can be learned in six months. The actual development of brazing skills varies with two major influences—the skill or training of the builder and, most important, the number of frames that have been built in a specific time period. For instance, Bruce learned his brazing skills while brazing 20 to 25 frames per week for Albert Eisentraut. How long would it take to develop the mysterious, or hard to define, *touch* if a builder only builds 20 to 25 per year? The interval between frames may be too long to provide adequate feedback.

Although Bruce has not had a long history of riding experience, his contact with riders has aided him in solving design problems. He cautions mail-order customers to be very careful in taking their measurements for their custom frame. Jokingly, he told us he would like to have a wax museum because he could fill it with unbelievable examples of mankind if some of the measurements he has received were true. Fortunately, he spends a great deal of time checking the measurements for plausibility before he begins to design the appropriate frame. Bruce's second concern involves the inability of some customers to describe the type of bicycle that they desire. For instance, Bruce frequently receives orders from customers who request a "stiff" frame. But, how stiff is "stiff"? To the owner of a touring frame with light-gauge tubing almost anything would be stiff. The opposite is true of a rider who requests a bike that is stiffer than his Cinelli track bike. Any prospective customer should define his desires in comparison to known quantities.

Like most of the better American builders, Bruce Gordon specializes in designing and building the perfect frame for a specific individual and his or her specific use. He builds tandems or singles, racing or touring frames. Most important to the tourist, Bruce builds his own touring racks which are designed to complement his touring frame geometry.

Proteus Design
9225 Baltimore Boulevard
College Park, MD 20740

Proteus Design was conceived in the late 1960s by three bicycle enthusiasts. What started out as a bicycle store, has evolved into a frame-building shop producing seven different models which include both touring and racing styles.

Barry Konig has been the prime motivator and driving force behind the development of Proteus Design. Since he and his partners were very young when they first opened the doors of Proteus Design, their imagination created a Dr. Paul Proteus with whom the bicycle industry could deal and feel confident that Proteus Design was a mature and businesslike establishment—not one, as Barry puts it, "run by a bunch of young punks." To this day the charade is continued, however, Barry freely admits that Dr. Paul Proteus exists only in their hearts. Reaching his thirties, and having spent 10 years in the bicycle business, Barry feels that the quality of his work speaks for itself.

The original owners of Proteus Design decided to build frames since their bicycle shop was thriving and they were looking for another challenge. They were mechanically inclined and felt confident that they could produce an acceptable product. Their initial step was to depart for England and try to apprentice to a builder, although the best they managed was a three-week stint at the Falcon factory in England in 1973. Barry says that they learned a lot in those three weeks and upon their return they commenced building their own frames. Of the three original owners, only Barry remains actively involved in the business, but even Barry does not build frames anymore. He, however, has helped train many of the frame builders that Proteus has employed in the past five years. Presently, the head of the frame shop trains all new frame builders in the Proteus design philosophy.

What is the Proteus method of frame building? Proteus Design incorporates the use of a lathe in mitering tubes for two reasons. The lathe expedites the operation and makes a precision cut at the same time. Barry believes "the strength (in a frame) comes from the joint and not so much from the lug, therefore mitering must be exact." He believes that 100 percent accuracy can only come by using a mitering machine.

He also believes that the best kind of fork crown is a semi-sloping investment cast crown. Proteus had been using various brands of crowns but Barry decided that they could eliminate some quality control problems by having an American firm make the fork crowns. Consequently, Proteus designed its own crown along the lines of the Cinelli semi-sloping crown, and subcontracted the design to an American company. The Proteus investment cast semi-sloping crown presently is used almost exclusively. Besides the fork crown, Proteus also has various brazed-on fittings, such as fork tangs, water bottle mounts, and brake cable stops, made to what Barry calls "our own exacting specifications."

Silver brazing rod is used exclusively on all Proteus frames because of its lower brazing temperature. On the rear dropouts, however, where the area to be filled often exceeds .003 inch (the properties of silver braze will not insure a strong joint when the area that is to be filled is larger than .003 inch), brass is used.

All frames are built exclusively with Reynolds tubing and Proteus stocks many of the different gauges, thus giving the customer a wide variety to choose from. Barry prefers Prugnat lugs and stocks them in 71-, 73-, and 75-degree sizes. By stocking

Figure 18-8: One of the four or five frame builders at Proteus Design. Here shown reaming out the bottom bracket chainstay opening.

the three different sizes, only a small amount of bending is required to suit the wide range of angles found on Proteus frames. Different seat clusters are used on the various models although Barry personally believes that the Italian fastback is the strongest.

Painting is done on the premises. Each frame receives a coat of Du Pont epoxy primer followed by a topcoat of Du Pont Imron available in 100 different colors. Both coats are baked on to further prevent chipping.

Proteus Design is different than all the American builders that we have featured in this chapter. None of the other builders we have included own their own bicycle shop. All are strictly frame builders. Proteus, on the other hand, started out as a bicycle shop that went into frame building in 1973 as an expansionary measure of the bicycle store. All the other frame builders in this chapter build one-of-a-kind frames whereas Proteus seldom does. Proteus is primarily geared to produce a semi-mass produced frame. With the way their tubes are precut and mitered ahead of time, they cannot vary the design greatly in order to custom-build a frame. However, they can build a frame that will satisfy the average frame customer in far shorter time than the small custom builders who usually have a very long waiting list for their products. Proteus Design is the national distributor of Reynolds tubing. They supply many braze-on sundries to other frame builders and they are the only builders in the United States that are currently authorized to build with Reynolds 753.

CHAPTER 19

General Observations: The American vs. the European Frame Builder

In the previous chapters, we examined some of the most famous builders in the world, their methods, philosophies, and their histories. One objective of this book is to take the "mystery" out of the custom frame. In order to accomplish that, we visited the builders, examined their techniques and, using a detailed outline, attempted to find each builder's answers to a list of technical questions. To put the answers in the proper perspective, we presented as much historical information as we were able to obtain. We feel, as we hope you do, that the builder's background can greatly influence our acceptance (or rejection) of his opinions. For instance, would you feel more comfortable with the design opinions of a successful ex-professional racer who has been building frames for 20 years, or the opinions of a person who has built only a few frames but has considerable skill in advertising his product? As we indicated in the introduction of this book, we have tried to minimize our biases and opinions. Instead, we have tried to build a framework of facts to better enable you to form your own opinions.

To this point, we have covered the basic methods of frame building, the parts that go together to complete a frame, and have reviewed the strengths and weaknesses of the parts. We then presented an inside look at many prominent builders. This chapter is devoted to a general summary of our opinions.

When we started our research, we felt it important to include information about American builders. Most important for several reasons, and most obvious, is their proximity. In some cases, there is a frame builder in your own town. The problems of dealing with someone overseas can be entirely eliminated. This leads, however, to another important reason to cover American builders. *Some of the builders are unqualified to build frames for public use. Some of their design theories are unsound as are their methods of construction.* Unfortunately, we were unable to arrive at a meaningful analysis of the U.S. builders because of the limited basis for objective evaluation. The primary problem is the short time that most American builders have been in operation. As we mentioned earlier, several builders went out of business between the time we started and finished the project!

European Strengths

Although many of the Europeans call the American builders "90-day wonders," some of our builders have accumulated years of experience. Few, however, have been building frames prior to the bicycle boom of 1973. Even though we have little historical information with which to judge our builders, let's take a look at how they compare with the Europeans.

As expected, the Europeans have time on their side. Most of the famous builders have more years of building experience than the total ages of our builders. In some instances, there is no substitute for experience. On the other hand, some of the builders never learned anything new after their first year in business. A substantial number of European builders have not changed their techniques because "that's the way I learned it."

On the whole, the American builder is more experimental and tends to branch out from the traditional methods. Unfortunately, this experimentation is not always founded on accepted cycling principles. We have seen several frames that were designed and built by American builders that followed general bicycle design theory but lacked the practicality that comes from experience. *For instance, some builders have made frames with chainstays that are so short that the tire must be deflated to remove (or install) the rear wheel!* Others have designed extremely attractive rear seatstay clusters that are elegantly designed but technically unsound. The ability of the Americans to innovate is best shown by the widespread use of Du Pont Imron paint. Several American builders use only Imron paint because of its incredible resistance to chipping.

The Italians appear to be the prime innovators in cycling. It is interesting to note, however, that they have purchased the manufacturing rights of several products designed by Pino Morroni of Detroit, Michigan. With the notable exception of Gerald O'Donovan of TI Raleigh, the Italians are responsible for the majority of the latest quality racing equipment. The Italians have the closest alliance with the professional bicycle racers who provide the "field testing." The Italian frame builders are generally considered to be the leading experts of interpreting a racer's needs and building a bicycle for those needs. On the other hand, the Italians have little interest in designing or producing top-quality touring bicycles. Any of the leading Italian frame builders can explain why a cast bottom bracket is important in a sprint or why the Italian section fork blade (called the continental section by TI Reynolds) is preferred for criteriums; but none can tell you how to attach panniers! Even in the United Kingdom, where there is greater emphasis on touring frames, the majority of the top-class touring frames are exported to the United States.

Innovations for Touring

Although the Europeans have decades of racing experience, they have spent little time engineering and building top-quality touring framesets. The use of a lightweight top-quality bicycle for touring is a new concept developed in the United States. Some of the most innovative touring products (like Eclipse touring bags) were developed in this country to respond to the recently created demand.

The reluctance of top-rated racers to use American framesets (excluding Schwinn) is partially attributable to the lack of racing experience of the American builder. On the other hand, the American builder has had great appeal to the tourist. Unlike the average tourist, the experienced racer usually understands the basics of proper bicycle positioning. The tourist usually has not been exposed to proper bicycle setup or riding technique. His or her main concern is the responsiveness of the builder to their requests for braze-on pannier fittings and special attachments.

Where did the famous builders get their experience in frame building? As reviewed in the individual historical chapters, many builders learned the art from an experienced family member or they were accepted as an apprentice. One American builder that we know of gained some experience in the United Kingdom: Matthew Assenmacher worked at JRJ Cycles. We were unable to find anyone in this country that had served as an apprentice in

France or Italy. The majority of the American builders learned from the "school of hard knocks."

The small European frame builders have another advantage over the Americans—their proximity to the major suppliers. Much of the developmental work for new products is performed by the major component manufacturers. For instance, when Cinelli designed his "new bicycle," Nisi made prototype 26-inch (66.7 cm.) rims and Clement made 26-inch tubulars. How many American builders can utilize the virtually unlimited resources of TI Reynolds, A. L. Colombo, and Campagnolo? The American frame builder obtains "new" components only after they have passed years of testing in Europe. Consequently, until the United States develops experienced component manufacturers, we will always be in the position of "following the leader."

In most cases, we found complete cooperation with every builder we spoke to. Generally, we were given a tour of their facilities, explanations of the assembly processes, and detailed descriptions of the parts used. Only specific brazing compounds (most particularly silver solder) and exact brazing temperature information was withheld. Why? Virtually every master builder considers the brazing technique as the most important feature of a frame. To our surprise, one American builder refused to describe (or let us photograph) his assembly jig. He apparently believes that his jig is more important than design or brazing techniques.

Art and Technology

The Americans are technically oriented. The Europeans view frame building as an art. Most of the builders seemed to be motivated primarily by the desire to create a quality product. In many cases the profit motive appeared secondary. In the United States, the number of builders has increased dramatically since the bicycle boom. It is quite the opposite in Europe. Many of the European builders complained of their inability to interest young apprentices in the art of frame building. Most explained that a frame builder will never become rich because of the extensive amount of hand detailing that is required to produce a top-quality frame. We also found it interesting that some totally inexperienced American builders charged as much for their frames as those produced by some of the "old pros" who had been in business for 30 years! We presume that the builder must have decided on his necessary profit margin or he feels that a price that is lower than that of the most famous European builders would imply inferior quality. It is essential, for anyone who intends to purchase a custom frame, to investigate the reputation of the builder. There is no guarantee of quality simply because known lugs and tubing are used or because the price is high.

The best equipment in the world won't help if improper brazing techniques are used. We have personally seen dozens of "basement" frames that have little more than quality components and a good paint job. Recently, at a Squaw Valley, California, training camp, a frame came apart during a minor crash. The tubes pulled out of the lugs on impact! When we spoke with ex-professional racer Tim Mountford, he informed us that a similar incident had occurred with another frame made by the *same* American builder! Unfortunately, there are no current means of controlling the quality of independent builders. We agree with Tim when he says, "Any bicycle put on the road should meet certain minimum standards." The question is: Who will make or enforce those standards?

We do not feel that it would be appropriate to make recommendations on which builders are "good"or "bad." The evaluation is not simple. We hope by presenting the technical opinions of the experts, that we have helped to contribute to a good decision on your part. Before you buy a frame, check into the credentials of the builder. Don't be misled by the builder's advertising. For instance, we saw an advertisement that suggested the consumer should consult the builder's design department for advice. Our analysis determined that the firm had only one employee, and he had built less than 25 frames in his lifetime! When you evaluate a frame, consider the time-tested success of the Europeans. Any innovation, whether European or American, should be evaluated solely on its merits. Even some of the most interesting ideas (like Cinelli *Bivalent* hubs) are no longer with us. Be analytical. Evaluate the skill and experience of the person building your next bicycle. If the builder effectively combines the experience of the masters with the ideas of the true innovators, you can be assured of an optimum bicycle for your individual needs.

A final question regarding frame design: "What qualifies you, as a rider, to properly design a frame?" The question is not meant to discredit you. The question is meant to direct the design responsibility to the proper person—the qualified builder. You may remember that several of the builders who were interviewed indicated that they preferred to build a frame from the customer's specifications. Even some of the most famous master builders recognize that their skills lie in the building process, not the process of interpreting the individual's sizing requirements. Every builder could tell us the relationship for the length of the top tube to each corresponding frame size. Fewer builders, however, were able to categorically state exactly how they compensated for a rider with a disproportionately long torso. If the experienced builder doesn't feel qualified to make sizing judgements, how can the average rider feel qualified? The relationship between cycling coach and frame builder is a complex one. Although we feel comfortable discussing most elements of cycling, we do not pretend to know how to design a frame that is "right" for each individual. Consequently, if you feel that your physique requires a special frame design, we recommend contacting a builder who specializes in fitting the frame to the rider. *Let the expert determine the design.* Fortunately, most of us will be able to comfortably fit on a bicycle that is designed for the "average" build. The important design criterion becomes the handling of the bicycle.

The following chapters cover the next logical step in a progression—using the information to most efficiently ride the bicycle as it was designed. Hopefully, the technical information and theory will provide a basis for understanding the "whys and wherefores of proper bicycle setup." An awareness of proper bicycle setup should assist you in making design decisions.

So far, we have presented definitions, and construction and design opinions of the prominent experts. The following chapter should provide the final link in the frame information chain for most cyclists—proper bicycle setup. For those who are considering the purchase of a new frame, the book should provide an insight into the advantages and disadvantages of the components in a frame and, hopefully, it will answer many of the questions that were unanswered by the average bicycle shop. We hope that the information will assist you in deciding the specifications of your next frame. For those of you who are lucky enough to already own your dream bicycle, we hope that the following information will better enable you to enjoy it.

PART VI

Putting the
Bicycle Together

CHAPTER 20

Bicycle Setup

This chapter covers "how to" correctly set up the bicycle; it does not include adjustments required to maximize the benefits of an individual's "style." Fine tuning is covered in chapter 21.

The basic design of the bicycle has remained unchanged for the last 75 years because it has been refined to the point that it maximizes the use of the human body. Although there have been many experiments involving alternative positions (reclining), the standard "bent over" position remains the most efficient. Let's take a look at why the bicycle is designed the way it is, and more importantly, how to set up the bicycle so that it most efficiently complements *your particular* physique.

Why the bent over position on a 10-speed? Most people will answer, "reduced wind resistance." While that statement is correct, it is not the only reason. If it were, the recumbent bicycle would be the "best" design. The primary reason for the "bent over" design can best be demonstrated using a bathroom scale. If you were to place one foot on the scale and press down with all your effort, how much weight would the scale register? Probably not more than 50 to 75 percent of your body weight. Now try the same experiment with the scale next to a wall. Attach a pair of handlebars to the wall, three feet from the floor. Grab the handlebars with your hands and press down on the scales with your foot. The increased leverage gained by using the combined strength of your hands, arms, back, and shoulder muscles will cause the scales to read in excess of your body weight. Since bulk power is not the sole factor governing cycling efficiency, the designs over the years modified the bicycle to best utilize the advantages of leverage while also considering the factors of fatigue, comfort, and wind resistance.

Do not vary from the following unless you have ridden according to the recommended setup for a considerable time and feel that a minor change will better fit your individual style or anatomy.

Adjusting the Bicycle

Saddle

STEP 1—*Adjust the saddle for proper horizontal angle*

Use a yardstick (figure 20-1) and adjust the *saddle angle* so that the front of the seat is slightly higher than the rear of the seat. Although it seems that the adjustment would be uncomfortable, this position will tend to keep the rider from sliding forward on the saddle. A saddle that is tilted downward in front will cause increased wrist, arm, and shoulder fatigue due to the need for constant pressure to maintain the position in the saddle. In some situations, a female rider may find this position uncomfortable. If the discomfort persists after 200 to 300 miles of riding, the tip of the saddle should be lowered until it is level or tilted slightly downward. After 500 to 1,000 miles of additional riding, muscles will develop which should enable her to tilt the saddle upward to its correct position.

STEP 2—*Saddle height*

Correct *saddle height* is an area of considerable dispute; however, most experts generally agree upon the correct starting point. The correct height is determined by sitting on the bicycle with both *heels* on the pedals (have someone hold you up). The seat is at the correct height when there is a slight bend in the knee (figure 20-2) at the bottom of the stroke. It is recommended that both heels be on the pedals during this adjustment because of the normal tendency to "favor" the leg that is extended. This usually results in the rider leaning to that side during the adjustment and consequently setting the saddle position too high. As a check, pedal backwards (both heels still on the pedals). Your hips should not sway. If they do, the saddle is too high.

The saddle height adjustment recommended here is set up for optimum pedaling performance. During our interviews with

Figure 20-1: Setting saddle angle. The front of the saddle should be slightly higher than the back of the saddle. Placing a yardstick on the saddle makes this critical adjustment easier to set. *Never allow the tip of the saddle to be lower than the back of the saddle.*

Figure 20-2: Setting saddle height. The saddle height should be adjusted with the rider on the bicycle with *both* heels on the pedals. Adjust the height of the saddle to allow for a *slight* bend in the knee at the bottom of the stroke. Quick Check: Pedal backwards with both heels on the pedals. If the hips sway, the saddle is too high.

Figure 20-3: Horizontal adjustment of the saddle. The saddle position from front to back is adjustable to compensate for individual variances in upper leg length and riding style. To correctly adjust the saddle, sit on the bicycle with both feet in the toe clips. The saddle is correctly adjusted when a plumb line from the center of the knee falls through the pedal axle of the foot when it is in the forward position with the crank parallel to the ground.

many experienced cycling coaches we found *no one* who felt that a formula based on leg length should determine the proper seat height. Proper pedaling techniques are discussed in chapter 22 and the saddle height modifications required by varying pedaling styles are also covered. In the majority of cases, however, this method will be correct. As a further guide, the tip of the saddle will generally be approximately 6 inches from the top of the top tube if the frame has been sized properly. That will increase slightly for very tall persons and decrease slightly for short persons.

STEP 3—*Horizontal saddle adjustment (front and rear)*

This adjustment is one of the least understood in cycling. It is *not* used to correct for differences in top tube length or to make up for a handlebar stem that is too long or too short. The horizontal saddle adjustment is designed to accommodate varying styles of riding (dealt with in chapter 22) and differences in individual variance in *thigh length*. The height of the saddle corresponds to the overall length of the rider's leg—the horizontal saddle adjustment corresponds to the size of the rider's thigh. Some people have very long thighs and correspondingly short shins while others have very long shins and short thighs. In other words, the horizontal saddle adjustment is used to insure the proper angle of thrust of the leg.

To set up the horizontal saddle position, sit on the bicycle with both feet in the toe clips. Rotate the cranks until they are parallel to the ground. Have a helper drop a plumb line from the center of your knee of the forward leg. The plumb line should extend through the pedal axle.

Toe Clips

The length of the toe clip is determined by the length of the foot. Usually toe clips come in three sizes: small, medium, and large. You can identify the size of the Christophe toe clip by the engraving on the top. The small toe clip is marked Christophe D; the medium is marked Christophe; and the large is marked

Christophe Special. A rough guide (variations are discussed in chapter 22) is:

Men's Shoe Size	Toe Clip Size
5–7	small
8–10	medium
11–13	large

Generally, the toe clip is the correct size if the ball of the foot is directly over the pedal axle. Men's sizes are the only ones listed here since bicycle pedals are one of the many bicycle components that are *not* designed for women. If the rule of placing the ball of the foot is maintained on the smaller woman's foot (ladies' shoe size 6½ or smaller), a small toe clip would be too big! The disadvantages are not immediately obvious; however, they are discussed in chapter 22.

When the toe clip is attached to the pedal (and the shoe cleat attached to the shoe), it should be adjusted so that the rider is pedaling slightly pigeon-toed. This results in a natural tendency to keep the knees close to the top tube which results in the most efficient pedaling motion and the least wind resistance. The reason for the pigeon-toed adjustment can be best demonstrated off the bike. Stand with both feet parallel, 8 inches apart, with the knees bent. In this position the knees will be slightly apart. If the toes are moved outward (figure 20-4B), the distance between the knees will increase. If the toes are pointed inward, the knees will come together. Obviously the feet should not be severely angled. If the toe clips are positioned too far out on the pedals, the rider's ankles will frequently hit the crankarms.

When the toe clips are inserted on the pedals, make sure that the buckle end is on the bottom so that the buckle does not rest on the side of the foot. Make sure that the strap has been twisted through the pedal (figure 20-5). This twisting eliminates strap movement each time the strap is tightened.

Figure 20-4A: This position does not encourage the "knees to the bar" aerodynamic position.

Figure 20-4B: If the feet of a rider are pointed *out*, the knees will also point out. Obviously incorrect.

Figure 20-4: Positioning shoe cleats and toe clips. The proper position for shoe cleat placement is best illustrated away from the bicycle. The cleats and toe clips should be mounted in such a way that the rider's knees remain close to the top tube when pedaling. If the feet of a rider are pointed straight ahead, the knees will also point straight ahead (figure 20-4A).

Figure 20-4C: If the feet are pointed *in*, the knees will point in. Although this is an exaggeration of the correct position, the cleats should be mounted to position the foot with the toes pointed *slightly* inward. The cycling shoe should *not* make actual contact with the front of the toe clip. It should be positioned ¼ inch behind the clip.

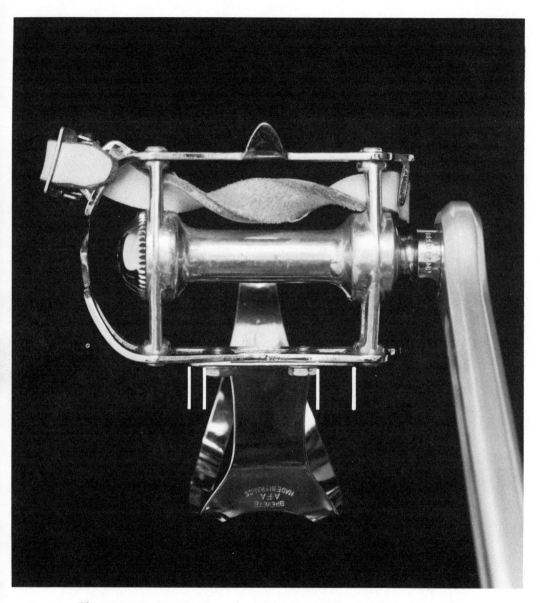

Figure 20-5: Positioning the toe clip and strap. The toe clip should be adjusted so that the toe of the shoe fits between the large opening in the front of the toe clip. If the cleats are mounted properly, the toe clip will be toward the *inside* of the pedal (note the adjustment slots where the clip attaches to the pedal). To eliminate toe strap slippage when tightening the strap, *twist* the strap through the pedal.

Figure 20-6: Determining stem length. Some people believe that the length of a handlebar stem can be determined by placing the elbow on the tip of the saddle with the fingers extended. . . . This is *not true*. This measurement does not consider the overall length of the arm and body *combined*.

Handlebar Stem (Extension)

The height of the handlebars is adjusted with the handlebar stem. Unless an "adjustable" stem is used (not recommended since they tend to slip under hard use), the length of the stem must be determined prior to its purchase and installation. The stem length is the variable corresponding to individual differences in upper body measurements.

Do not buy a stem based on the relationship of your arm length and the distance from the tip of the saddle to the handlebars (figure 20-6). While this is a good starting point, it does not take into account the individual differences in forearm length versus overall arm length or length of the upper body.

Determine the proper stem length by raising the handlebars to approximately 1 inch lower than the saddle (exception—racing position for short-distance events). With the hands on the handlebars (figure 20-7), and the elbows bent slightly, the rider's nose should be approximately 1 inch behind the handlebars. Make sure you are sitting in a normal position on the saddle. This should be checked by someone who is standing away from the bicycle as explained in the saddle adjustment. If the plumb line from the nose is more than 1 inch behind the handlebars, the stem is too long. If the nose is ahead of the handlebars, the stem is too short. The handlebars should be adjusted so that the lower portion of the bar is slanting down slightly at the rear.

Now the bicycle is probably set up properly. But how do you check to make sure?

How to Check for Proper Positioning

Use an impartial observer to examine your position on the bicycle to see that the following rules apply to the way you are sitting on the bicycle.

Does the back have a smooth bend in the three basic handlebar positions (figures 20-7, 20-8, 20-9)? In no position should there be an acute bend in any area of the back. This sharp bend will usually result in back pain which can be virtually eliminated if the position is correct. Have your helper check each position while you keep your eyes looking ahead as if you were riding.

Figure 20-7: Determining length of the stem (handlebar Position 3). The stem is correctly sized if a plumb line from the nose drops approximately 1 inch behind the handlebars in Position 3. The elbows should be slightly bent. Notice that the back is *lower* than 45 degrees in Position 3. The rider's weight is comfortably divided—45 percent front, 55 percent rear. The arms are relaxed and the rider's weight is supported by the arms and shoulders combined. There are no acute bends in the back. (Note: The handlebar positions are numbered in anticipation of a more detailed discussion of the subject in chapter 22.)

Figure 20-8: Determining length of the stem (handlebar Position 2). A plumb line from the nose drops slightly further behind the handlebars. Again the weight is smoothly divided and there are no radical bends in the back. In handlebar Position 2, the back should be at or *slightly below* 45 degrees and the rider should be in a position to breathe efficiently.

Figure 20-9: Determining the length of the stem (handlebar Position 1). The rider's weight should again be comfortably divided. There should be no critical bends in the back and the rider should be able to breathe comfortably. The back should be above 45 degrees in handlebar Position 1.

Check Position 1 (figure 20-9). The back should have a smooth curve and should be above 45 degrees. No one is racing 100 percent all the time and therefore you should have a position that is efficient and comfortable. This position should be used for normal riding. If the back is not above 45 degrees, check to see if the saddle has been adjusted too far back, and check to see if the handlebar stem is too long. It may be possible that the top tube is too long.

Check Position 2 (figure 20-8). Again, the back should have a smooth curve. Your nose is approximately 1 inch behind the handlebars, and the angle of the back should be at, or below, 45 degrees. This is very important and many times does not occur if the frame has a top tube that is too short or a stem that isn't long enough. The importance of the 45-degree angle is simple but not universally understood—unless the back is below 45 degrees, the largest muscle in your body, the gluteus maximus or "rear end," is not fully utilized. This can be best demonstrated off the bicycle. Place one hand on your rear end and walk a few steps. You will notice that the muscle does not flex with each step—the majority of the muscle is not being used. Now bend over so that your back is less than 45 degrees and again walk with your hand on one "cheek." This time you will see that the whole muscle flexes with each step.

Check Position 3 (figure 20-7). The back should still have a smooth bend and the head should not have to be held up too high in order to see. Figures 20-10 to 20-13 demonstrate in exaggerated form the problems to avoid.

Having the bicycle properly adjusted is only part of sitting comfortably and efficiently on the bicycle. The following are general rules of good cycling "posture":

1. The rider should *always* keep his elbows slightly bent when riding. There are two reasons for this.
   a. Bent elbows act as shock absorbers over bumps. This results in less strain on the joints in the wrist, elbow, and shoulder, and less strain on the neck. It also reduces the tendency to "push" the bicycle into a bump or hole that cannot be avoided. The shock absorber effect will greatly reduce stress on the tires, wheels, and frame.

(continued on page 207)

Figure 20-10: Incorrect handlebar position. The hands are located too far toward the ends of the handlebars and the arms are stiff. All road shock is transmitted directly into the rider's body from the wrist to the shoulder. The arm is not acting as a shock absorber.

Figure 20-11: Incorrect handlebar position (short stem, Position 3). The rider's nose is ahead of the handlebars and too much weight is concentrated on the front wheel. The chest is constricted making breathing difficult. The rider has to spend a great deal of energy holding his head up to see where he is going because of the "bunched-up" position of his body.

Figure 20-12: Incorrect handlebar position (long stem, Position 2). The rider's weight is too spread out. Too much weight is placed on the front wheel. The rider supports himself without the help of his shoulders.

Figure 20-13: Incorrect handlebar position (long stem, Position 3). Again the rider is too stretched out and has too much weight over the front wheel. The rider's nose is 2 inches behind the handlebars. The arms are not used to assist the leg muscles—they are supporting the rider. The shoulders are not used effectively.

b. If the rider is ever bumped by another rider, the elbow can be flexed and the effect of the bump minimized. If the elbows are unyielding, the front wheel will swerve. To repeat, the elbows should be bent in all three handlebar positions. As you can see in figure 20-11, when the elbows are bent in Position 3 the rider is extremely low. This position should only be used for racing under extreme stress and/or riding against a stiff head wind. Frequently, riders who have frames that are too big use Position 3 all the time and ride with stiff elbows. This does not allow the benefits of the use of the arm, chest, and shoulder muscles nor does it provide the "over 45 degree" and "under 45 degree" differences covered in figures 20-7 to 20-9.

2. When using Position 3, the wrist should be held straight. This usually results in the hand being located near the curve in the handlebars. The reason for the straight wrist can best be explained by analogy. When a weight lifter picks up a heavy weight he adjusts his hand position so that the wrist is straight, providing the maximization of the strength of the joint. To place great stress on a bent wrist requires effort to keep the wrist bent—thereby reducing the effective use of strength. The use of the arm and shoulder in increasing efficiency is discussed in the beginning of this chapter.

If you are experiencing a problem in position, or simply want to double-check the setup of your bicycle, have a helper take a sideview picture of you on the bicycle in each of the three handlebar positions. Check the previously mentioned guides against your position.

Further assistance can be utilized from the pictures found in the bicycling magazines. Remember, however, that like any sport, many riders tend toward "fads," e.g., low handlebars, high handlebars, big frames, small frames. Don't look at a sprint position and wonder why it's different than your road position. You should look for riders who share your build. Then you can analyze how they sit on the bicycle. This sounds easier than it actually is since we have never seen captions for pictures that include the rider's height, weight, leg length, foot size, or arm length. This can be overcome, however, by using transparent graph paper.

Since we can be sure that the rider is using 27-inch wheels, all you have to do is determine a scale using the number of grids you have on the graph paper. It is a fairly simple matter to approximate all the important measurements. Also when the graph paper is laid over the picture, relationships such as nose over the handlebars, angle of arms reaching for the handlebars, angle of head, relationship of saddle adjustment, and angle of the back become very obvious. Does your position have the same relationships? Remember that the professional bicycle racer probably is more supple and consequently looks more relaxed. The graph paper is merely another means of taking the experience of a "master" and generalizing to your individual needs.

To double-check that all adjustments are correct, you should perform the following test. Before you begin the analysis you will need a bathroom scale and a stack of books that are equal in thickness to the height of the scale. Fill in the blanks of the chart as follows:

Place the front wheel of your bicycle on the bathroom scale. Place some books that have been stacked to the same height as the bathroom scale under the rear wheel. Take readings of the combined weight of you and your bicycle at the front and rear wheels. This process should be completed for each of the three handlebar positions. Make sure that you are sitting on the saddle in exactly the same position that you would normally sit when riding.

The percentage of weight on the front wheel will increase from handlebar Position 1 to Position 3. Conversely, the percentage of weight on the rear wheel will decrease from handlebar Position 1 to Position 3. Your overall weight distribution should be approximately 45 percent front to 55 percent rear in handlebar Position 3 if your bicycle is properly adjusted.

Weight Distribution Analysis

(Guide: 45 percent front to 55 percent rear)

Position of hands on handlebars	A Weight recorded at front wheel	B Weight recorded at rear wheel	C Total weight A plus B	D % of weight on front wheel A ÷ C	E % of weight on rear wheel B ÷ C
Position 1	_____ lbs.	_____ lbs.	_____ lbs.	_____ %	_____ %
Position 2	_____ lbs.	_____ lbs.	_____ lbs.	_____ %	_____ %
Position 3	_____ lbs.	_____ lbs.	_____ lbs.	_____ %	_____ %

To determine the percentage of weight on each wheel (D) and (E), take the weight recorded at the front wheel (A) and add it to the weight recorded at the rear wheel (B). Next, divide the weight at the front wheel (A) by the combined weight (C) which will result in the % of weight on the front wheel (D). To calculate the % of weight on the rear wheel, divide the weight on the rear wheel (B) by the total weight (C) which will result in the % of weight on the rear wheel (E).

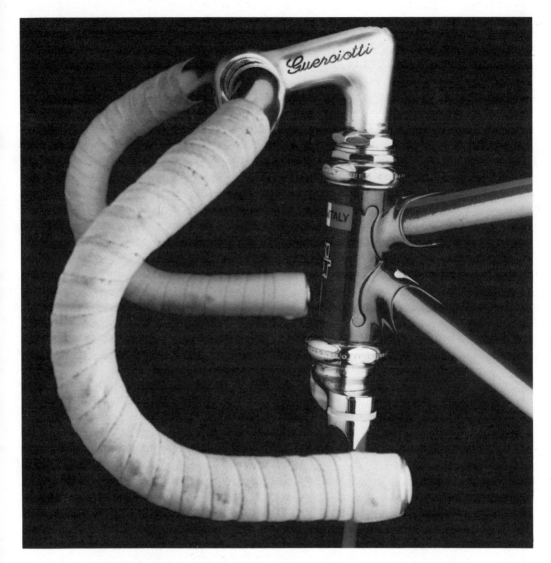

Figure 20-14: Correct handlebar stem adjustment. The handlebar stem should be placed far into the steering tube. If the stem is too high, the expander bolt will be located near the threaded section of the steering column. The normal stress on the stem will adversely affect the top of the steering column and it can break! The repair cost is substantial since a whole new fork would be required.

Figures 20-15, 20-16: The tape should be affixed to the top tube at the point where the handlebar touches the tube if the wheel is allowed to turn to its sidewards limit. The tape is useful for preventing paint damage while carrying the bicycle and, more importantly, it minimizes the possibility of *denting* (and weakening) the top tube in the event of a crash.

211

Fitting the Shorter Rider

The setup relationships described in this chapter will hold true for almost everyone. Although a person over 6′5″ is limited to a 25-inch or 26-inch frame (because most builders will not build a larger size), a suitable handlebar stem and seatpost can be obtained that will allow an efficient cycling position. Even basketball star Bill Walton, has been properly fitted for a bicycle. For several reasons, proper sizing of the bicycle becomes a serious problem when the rider is shorter than 5′2″.

The first and most important obstacle in accommodating the short person is faced in the physical limitations of designing a frame that is small enough. Stock frames rarely are found in less than the 19½-inch size because the top tube and down tube practically touch at the point where they join on the head tube. It is obvious, therefore, that the builder can only marginally reduce the frame size under 19½ inches. Some custom builders have gone to great lengths to join the top tube and down tube in an attempt to accommodate the small rider. Many times, however, it is impossible to design, or build, a "standard" frame that will allow proper cycling position for the short rider. A secondary problem in fitting small persons is the lack of components designed for the short person. This is because most bicycles and components are designed for the "average" male physique. Until recently, cycling has been a predominantly male sport and the cycling accessories have been designed accordingly. It is not entirely uncommon, however, to see a woman riding an all-Campagnolo lightweight bicycle in this country.

Let's take a look at the specific problems encountered by the short rider and review possible solutions to these problems.

Frame

The short rider finds it much more difficult to find a standard frame that will be comfortable (or even ridable in some cases) if the rider has disproportionately long or short legs. If the rider has very long legs, the reach to the handlebars will be too great. On the other hand, if the rider has a disproportionately long torso, the lowest saddle position may still be too high. A change in handlebars or saddle will have no effect since the frame tubes cannot be built any shorter. What next? We suggest talking to some of the custom builders who can design a frame that uses 24-inch wheels. Most people react negatively when first presented with the idea because they feel that no quality equipment is available for the 24-inch-wheel bicycle and that they are forced to ride a "child's" bicycle. If you are too short for a 19-inch frame and you are interested in a quality 10-speed, you owe it to yourself to examine some of the equipment that is available. We will concede that the equipment isn't readily available, but it does exist. For starters, try Paris Sport Cycle in Ridgefield Park, New Jersey. Their resident frame builder, Francisco Cuevas, builds top-quality lightweight frames in both standard and small sizes and the store carries 24-inch rims and tubular tires. They also carry most of the components necessary to complete a quality 24-inch-wheel 10-speed. Don't eliminate the 24-inch-wheel bicycle until you have looked at the "good" equipment. If you are a short rider that can "get by" on a 19-inch frame with a short handlebar stem and the saddle resting on the top tube, optimum cycling position may be improved with careful selection of the frame components.

Handlebars

A handlebar is considered to be the correct size if it is as wide as the rider's shoulders. If the bars are too narrow, breathing is restricted; if the bars are too wide (normally the situation for the small rider), the arms are inefficiently supporting the rider and causing increased wind resistance. The drop and reach of the handlebars may be too great for the small rider. Many riders are unaware that some handlebars come in various widths and bends. Measure the width of the handlebars before you purchase them; Cinelli handlebars, for instance, are available in 38-cm., 40-cm., and 42-cm. widths. If you are very small, you may want to investigate the good-quality alloy handlebars that have been designed for a bicycle with 24-inch wheels. With the correct width handlebars combined with a small stem, the short rider should be able to set up the bicycle for comfortable and efficient cycling.

Brake Levers

Similar to most quality cycling accessories, the brake levers are designed for the average male hand. This is an area that causes even more problems than oversize handlebars, since the potential for an accident is increased if the rider cannot easily manipulate the brake levers. There is a small amount of variation between the reach of most standard brake levers, so the search for a "small" reach lever may be unnecessary. There are two ways to attack this problem. The first is to increase the strength of your hands so that the brake lever can be used with only two or three fingers. Even riders with very small hands (women's glove size 5-6) can operate most levers after practice and exercise. The best and least expensive method to increase hand and finger strength is to regularly practice squeezing a tennis ball. If you are a rider whose hands are too small for brake retention with two or three fingers, you should contact a builder who carries 24-inch wheels and tires since he should be able to supply small brake levers that will fit the junior-size handlebars.

In most cases, going to the smaller, scaled-down equipment may not be entirely necessary. For instance, it may be necessary to use a 24-inch-wheel frame because of height and leg measurement, but narrow handlebars may not be necessary if the individual is broad shouldered. Equally true, smaller brake levers may not be necessary for someone who may need a 24-inch-wheel bicycle but who has large hands. Obviously, the equipment should match the rider's physical needs.

Saddle

Proper selection of a saddle *may* permit use of a 19-inch frame in the situation where the rider has very short legs, but adequate torso length to fit the standard-size frame. Generally, the plastic saddles (Cinelli Unica Nitor, for instance) have less height than the traditional leather saddle. Before you purchase the saddle, check the distance from the saddle's frame support rails to the top of the saddle itself. Often the plastic saddles are much shallower than their leather counterparts. The shallow saddle can effectively reduce the distance from the top of the saddle to the pedal by as much as an inch.

Careful selection of handlebars, stem, and saddle can increase comfort and efficiency, but one problem remains—how do we compensate for the rider's shorter legs and smaller foot size and their effect on pedaling efficiency?

Cranks

A *very* short person should consider cranks which are shorter than the standard 170 mm. How short? Unfortunately, we cannot provide a rule of thumb. In fact, in our discussion with Eddie Borysewicz, national cycling coach, he indicated that no one can unequivocably provide an answer. Because so little is known about optimum crank length, Eddie has considered devoting two or three years and his doctoral dissertation to the relationship between crank length and leg length! Small cranksets are available to those with very short legs, but only use the short cranks if you feel they are absolutely necessary since the accompanying chainwheels are usually too small to provide adequate *gear ratios* for the adult. We recommend that you do not vary crank length without the advice of a competent coach. Presuming that standard-size cranks will be used, let's turn our attention to one last item that must be utilized to assist in efficiently transmitting your energy into motion—pedals.

Pedals

Just like all other cycling components, pedals have been designed to fit the average male foot. Unfortunately, the adverse effect of an oversize pedal is much greater than a pair of handlebars that are too large. If the handlebars are too big, the rider will endure some discomfort; if the pedals are too big, the rider's pedaling motion will be very seriously affected. An analysis of one of the fine points of coaching should help clarify this point.

There are two basic extremes in pedaling style—the pusher (the rider that uses relatively high gears at low rpm's) and the pedaler (the rider who uses relatively low gears at relatively high rpm's). *Generally,* the pusher is a heavily muscled individual who utilizes brute strength instead of finesse. The inverse is true of the pedaler, who is usually of slight build and uses high pedal rpm's to maintain overall cycling speed. To maximize the effects of either of the two pedal styles, the toe clips and shoe cleats should be carefully adjusted. As a general rule, the pusher should have his foot deeper into the toe clip than the pedaler. That is, the ball of the foot of the pusher may be as much as ¼ to ⅜ inch *ahead* of the pedal axle. The pedaler should have his foot as much as ¼ to ⅜ inch *behind* the pedal axle.

Unfortunately, it logically follows that if the rider's foot is very small, the ball of the foot will always be ahead of the pedal axle even with a short toe clip! Use of the short Christophe toe clip on a standard-size pedal will not allow proper placement of a shoe smaller than a ladies' size 7. Therefore, without choice, the rider with small feet is forced to pedal like a pusher, regardless of his or her appropriate style. You should remember this analysis when buying pedals for your bicycle; most people are amazed at the amount of increased pedaling efficiency resulting from proper foot placement.

We have attempted to briefly cover the major obstacles encountered by the short person—the list is not all inclusive. We hope that these guidelines will help encourage the short rider to spend a little extra time in search of components that will provide optimal use of his or her individual physique.

Bicycle Setup for Touring

The basic features of a touring bike should be obvious to everyone who has read this far. So let's take a look at how to set up the bicycle to go touring.

The relationships of seat height, handlebar height, and stem length remain unchanged. The important difference between the problems encountered by the tourist versus the racer is the additional equipment that the tourist carries with him. The handling of the bicycle can be drastically affected by improper mounting of packs.

Although there are a large number of well-made lightweight packs made specifically for the cyclist, few of the designs consider the effects of the load on the operation of the bicycle. To understand the features necessary in a set of touring packs, let's look at the problems encountered with the addition of the packs to the bicycle.

If a bicycle is designed properly, it will be stable up to very high speeds. The frame design complements the suggested weight distribution of the rider (45 percent front—55 percent rear). In fact, the bicycle rolls easier and handles better when the weight is distributed 45 percent front—55 percent rear. It follows, therefore, that any equipment that is added to the bicycle should be distributed so that it complements the design criteria of the bicycle. For that reason, a bicycle will handle considerably better with 27 pounds of equipment over the front wheel and 33 pounds of equipment over the back wheel than it will with the same total weight (60 pounds) over the back wheel alone. In addition to the unbalanced condition, the rear tire, rim, and spokes will take much greater punishment if *all* of the weight is over the rear wheel of the bicycle.

The problem of stability is not totally solved by distributing the weight over the bicycle, however. Loosely mounted packs create unexpected forces on the bicycle that can lead to a serious crash. This is most evident in the situation where a loosely secured handlebar pack contains a heavy object—it is virtually impossible to steer the bicycle without overcorrecting. The problem of weight transfer is caused by two situations. First, a heavy object is packed without surrounding materials that will limit its ability to move, and second, by packs that do not have the means to be anchored securely to the bicycle.

While we feel that it's not appropriate to single out any manufacturers to illustrate the essentials to look for in touring equipment, we have included pictures of the unique Eclipse line of cycle touring bags.

Panniers

The panniers should be loaded with the heaviest items at the bottom. When equipment is packed it should be arranged so that routine cycling motions do not allow the contents to move. One way to reduce movement is to use a pannier that is not cut square on the bottom. A triangular bottom allows easy, solid placement of heavy objects. Remember, as in high-speed cornering, it is essential to keep the center of gravity of the bicycle as low as possible. The panniers should be supported by more than one or two stress points to reduce the potential for equipment failure. The mounting system should be adjustable to insure freedom of movement of the leg and optimum weight distribution.

Handlebar Packs

The pack should be solidly attached to the handlebars with the greatest possible amount of support for the bag. Few accidents are more serious than ones caused by loss of control of the steering

Figure 20-17: Proper frame loading for touring requires proportionate weight distribution and a system that minimizes the tendency of the packed materials to move.

or when a solid object becomes wedged in the front wheel. Presuming the bag is packed correctly, the most important consideration is anchoring the bag securely to eliminate movement. The Eclipse bag uses a unique shock cord arrangement that virtually eliminates movement. The importance of the proper attachment of a handlebar pack cannot be overemphasized—it is extremely difficult to control the bicycle *under ideal conditions* with a poorly mounted bag. In emergency situations, a marginally designed bag can drastically reduce the chances of escaping a crash.

Figure 20-18: Eclipse has designed a handlebar pack that is held virtually motionless by its two shock cord mounts.

CHAPTER 21

Assembling
the Bicycle

Proper assembly of your frame does not require special tools if the builder did everything perfectly. Unfortunately, this is not always the case. Very expensive special tools are required to properly mount the headset and bottom bracket, and very few bicycle shops have all the tools to properly assemble a quality frame. There is one alternative—order your frame with the headset and bottom bracket already installed. Unless the builder is careless, this eliminates the need to obtain the special tools required to face the head and bottom bracket. It also eliminates the need for you to worry about matching the threads and the width of the bottom bracket axle. The use of the Campagnolo tools to fit the headset and bottom bracket is covered in chapter 3.

Let's look at the specific steps in assembling the frame, presuming the headset and bottom bracket are properly installed. The steps required to attach Campagnolo components are discussed since the vast majority of top-quality frames are built and designed to fit Campagnolo parts.

Checking Frame Alignment

Always check frame alignment *before* attaching brakes, derailleurs, or other components. If the frame is out of line or has been twisted in shipping, and you decide to return it, the builder will not want to receive it with scratches where you have attached the many fittings that are required on a 10-speed. For this test, you will need a length of string and an accurate ruler.

Place one end of the string on the rear fork tip (where the wheel axle will be positioned) and run the string to the front of the bicycle. Run the string over the head and to the remaining rear fork tip. Have someone hold the string, under tension, in this position while you measure the distance between the string and the seat tube. The string should be equidistant from each side of the tube. If it isn't, you have a problem that can be corrected in two ways. First, you can return the frame to your dealer or the builder. Chances are, they will cold set (bend) the stays into alignment if the problem isn't too serious. If the frame is made out of Reynolds 753, you have to choose between accepting the frame the way it is or returning it to be rebuilt—753 cannot be cold set. If the frame is not 753 and the inaccuracy is minor, you can have an experienced bicycle shop cold set the misaligned stay without permanent damage to the frame if it is done properly. Unless you have had considerable experience bending lightweight framesets, *don't attempt to correct the problem yourself.* In cold setting framesets, you must have the experience to know exactly how far either to pull it out (or push it in) because the cold setting must be done in one motion to be most effective and to cause the least amount of permanent damage.

Assuming your frame passes the first test, use the same string and ruler for another check. This time the string should run between all four fork tips. That is, start at the rear tip, guide the string through the front fork tips and back to the remaining rear tip. Measurements taken from the seat tube to the string should be equidistant. If your frame passed the first check and flunked this test, the fork is probably twisted. Again, this is no job for you to tackle. Take the frame back. It is unlikely that your frame won't pass these two tests if you have purchased it from a first-class bicycle shop dealing with "name brand" frames or from a competent builder. It is possible, however, that the frame was damaged during shipping. Furthermore, these tests are useful to check for hidden damage to your frame after a crash.

Checking Fork End Alignment

This test is easily performed with special tools, but it is possible to check for problems without them. Any problem found, however, is easily corrected only with the right tools. (See chapter 3.)

If you have access to the special tools, attach the right and left tool on the front fork. You should note that the front fork tips are

(continued on page 224)

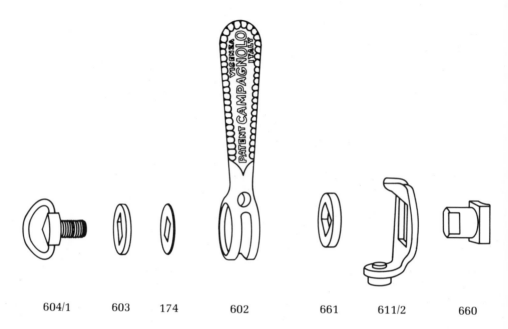

604/1   603   174   602   661   611/2   660

Figure 21-1: Exploded view of derailleur parts ready for assembly. Once you have prepared the frame (filing the excess paint from the derailleur braze-on bosses), then you are ready to assemble the derailleur control levers. On the derailleur lever bosses (part #660), which have been brazed on by the builder, you assemble the parts in the following order: control lever plate (#611/2 on the left and #600/2 on the right), brazed boss collar (part #661), control lever (#602 on the left and #601 on the right), lever friction plate (part #174), cover plate (part #603), and friction-adjusting wing nut (part #604/1). All these parts can also be purchased as a set—#1013/5 left (front changer) braze-on control and #1013/6 right (gear) braze-on control.

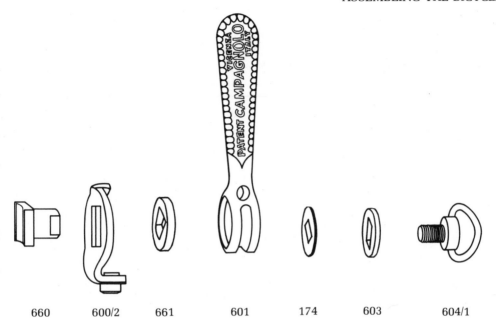

660   600/2   661   601   174   603   604/1

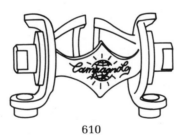

610

If your frame has derailleur braze-on bosses and you want to use the Campagnolo twin down tube lever, you will first have to detach the control lever plates from the clip (part #610). In so doing, you will end up destroying the clip, making it impossible to use in the future. If you do not want to do this, the same results can be attained by purchasing the control lever plates (parts #611/2 and #600/2) separately. In both of the above methods, you will also have to purchase an additional washer as shown in this illustration.

inserted inside the spacer that floats freely on the tool itself. If the fork tips are perfectly aligned, the edge of the tool will be 1 mm. apart, *all the way around the tooled surface.* A large proportion of factory-built frames are *not!* There is no cause for alarm unless the inaccuracy is very large. Simply use the tool to bend the fork tips into proper alignment (make sure the tool is tight). The exact same test is performed on the rear tips, but the spacers are placed inside the fork tips. If the tools are 1 mm. apart, the rear tips are exactly 121 mm. apart.

If you do not have access to the tools, use a pair of wheels that include a set of known quality hubs. For instance, the quality control of the Campagnolo hubs is so consistent that unless someone has substituted the number of washers or damaged the hub, it will be as close to perfect as you need to worry about. Insert the hub into the fork in the normal fashion but *do not* tighten the quick-release lever. If the forks must be spread to insert the hub, they will have to be adjusted. Also, this is obviously true if you must squeeze the forks together to insert the hub.

Look very closely at the clearance between the fork tip and the locknuts on the axle. The fork tip should be exactly parallel to the flat surface of the locknuts—if they aren't, some adjustment will be required. The quick-release wheel should fit into the fork tips without any stretching or twisting at all.

Assuming everything is okay so far, you are ready to add the components to the frame. Since this is not intended to be a basic bicycle repair book, we will cover only problems that may be experienced if you are selecting and fitting your choice of components.

Attaching Derailleur Levers

If you do not have braze-on derailleur lever bosses, simply attach the twin down tube control lever. On frames that include the brazed-on derailleur lever boss, you will have some work to do before the levers can be mounted.

First, in most cases, you must remove the paint *from the boss portion only.* If you are not careful with the removal of the paint, you can very easily scratch the paint on the down tube. To mount the control lever, you need to install Campagnolo parts nos. 611/2 and 600/2 (left- and right-hand braze-on control lever plate). If your local bicycle shop does not carry the parts, you can use the parts that are already built into the twin control clip. To remove the parts, however, you will be required to destroy the clip. Assemble the controls with the washers in the same sequence as shown in the illustration. No other problems should be encountered in mounting the remaining parts of the derailleurs.

Mounting Brakes

You should tell the builder which type of brake you intend to install. If you are buying a frame off the rack, make sure that you match the brakes with the design of the frame. Most builders construct their frames for the popular 52-mm. brake. Some builders of racing bicycles will build a frame to accept the 47-mm. brake. These brakes are not interchangeable even with the use of a drop bolt for the rear.

Many riders that are using the sidepull brake have experienced the problem of one brake shoe making contact with the wheel rim before the other. As they try to correct this problem, they quickly find that adjusting the center bolt has no effect. On the Campagnolo brake, the calipers can be centered by inserting the thin Campagnolo cone wrench (13 mm.) on the flats of the center bolt adjacent to the frame. The wrench is used to center the calipers and maintain the position of the nut as the center bolt is tightened.

For other sidepull brakes, which do not include the machined surfaces, an effective but crude method is used. Place a machinist's punch on the brake spring of the caliper that is farthest from the rim. Give the punch a tap with a hammer until the calipers are equidistant.

Inserting the Seatpost

It is impossible to say with certainty what the correct seatpost size is for your frame. It is important to size the post properly since a post that is slightly too big can be badly scratched and a post that is too small can sometimes slip or it can place unnecessary stresses on the seat lug. The following is a

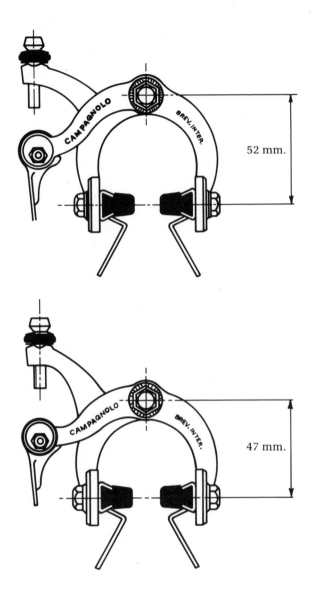

Figure 21-2: Be certain that the brakes you intend to use will fit the frame size. While most builders construct frames to accept 52-mm. brakes, some frames accept only the 47-mm. size.

general guide to be used as a starting point in selecting the correct seatpost:

Possible Sizing

Country of manufacture	Frame with double-butted tubing (in mm.)	Frame without double-butted tubing (in mm.)
Italy	26.8, 27.0, 27.2	26.2
France	26.2, 26.8	26.2, 26.4
England	27.0, 27.2	26.2, 26.8

Handlebar and Stem Compatibility

Two problems are encountered with handlebar and stem compatibility. The first is the different specifications that do not allow interchanging brands of handlebars and stems, and second, the varying dimensions of fork column diameters that do not allow total compatibility of fork columns and stems.

Generally speaking, it is best to maintain the same brand of handlebar and stem. TTT bars and stem *are* interchangeable with Cinelli bars and stems; however, the Japanese Gran Compe and SR stems *will not* interchange with either the TTT or Cinelli handlebars.

When checking interchangeability between stems and headsets, the French are usually the exception. The Italian, English, and the Japanese stems are 22.2 mm. and fit the Campagnolo headset with Italian or English threads. The French stems are 21.85 mm. and unless used with French headsets, or a Campagnolo headset with French threads, do not permit an acceptably tight fit.

Bottom Bracket

If the bottom bracket of your frame is drilled, or cut out, you should ensure that the bearings are protected from dirt and water by a protective sleeve like Campagnolo part nos. 2110/1 and 2110.

Figure 21-3: The plastic protective sleeve is designed to fit inside the bottom bracket on bicycles which have a cutout bottom bracket shell. The sleeve will protect the precision bearings from dirt and water during normal use.

Hub Interchangeability

Just as all hubs are not of equal quality, they are not all the same size. You should tell your builder what type of hubs you plan to use. Most builders presume the use of Campagnolo hubs and build the forks with a 101-mm. space and the rearstays with a 121-mm. space. Few hubs besides the Campagnolo offer all three threads (Italian, French, and English) for the freewheel. The top-quality Japanese hubs are usually 100 mm. front and 120 mm. rear, like Campagnolo. The lower-priced Japanese hubs are often 96 mm. front and 124 mm. rear. The

French hubs are often 96 mm. front and 122 mm. rear. The frame should be built and aligned for the hubs to be used, otherwise the chain line will be inaccurate. Although the widths of the Japanese and the Campagnolo hubs are the same, they are not perfectly interchangeable. There will be a very slight difference in chain-lines if the hubs are interchanged. In appendix V, we have included proper chain line specifications. To correct minor chain line deficiencies, you can use Campagnolo freewheel spacers (part no. 651) which come in three sizes: 1, 1.5, and 2 mm.

Advise your builder in advance, if you plan to use a 6-speed freewheel—it requires a 126-mm. rearstay opening.

CHAPTER 22

Riding Techniques

While it is very difficult to "coach" a rider without being familiar with his or her individual style, there are some basic rules of thumb which generally have universal application.

Gear Selection

Countless pages have been written about gear selection: for mountains, the flats, racing, training; but in the final analysis, the "correct gear" depends on the specific anatomy and style of the rider. Stocky, heavily muscled individuals tend to pedal larger gears at lower rpm's than slim, lightly muscled persons. But, what is the correct gear for you?

Generally, a rider should attempt to pedal between 80 to 100 rpm's on a tubular-tired, lightweight bicycle and 60 to 80 rpm's on a clincher tire bicycle. The recommended rpm's vary because of the difference in the revolving weight of the wheels which affects your pedaling speed. Variations within that range will reflect individual anatomy, conditioning, and how much practice at pedaling the rider has had. The argument in support of high pedal rpm's with a "low" gear is simple—the rider will be able to ride longer. Let's look at an exaggerated analogy to clarify this point. Which exercise could you best perform: lifting a 2-pound weight with one hand over your head 50 times, or lifting 100 pounds with one hand over your head once? This analogy is not perfect since it does not take the time expended into account. It does, however, demonstrate the point that a muscle is only capable of exerting a limited amount of force and, most importantly, the muscle can be conditioned to perform a large number of light repetitions in a shorter period of time than it takes to condition the muscle to double or triple the amount of force exerted. Accepting the fact that "high rpm's" are desirable, we arrive at the problem of defining "how high is high?"

> *Rule of thumb:* If the gear you have selected is too high, your legs will fatigue before your lungs. If the selected gear is too low, your lungs will fatigue first.

This rule can easily be verified by performing two test rides. First, select the lowest gear on your bicycle. Pedal as fast as you can and maintain that pace for 15 seconds. You will notice that your legs will not be tired, however, your lungs will be "burning." After resting, perform the second test. Select the highest gear on your bike and again pedal as fast as you can for 15 seconds. Your lungs will not be "burning," instead, your legs will feel "tight." Practice using this rule of thumb to maximize your output whenever you ride. If you experience abnormal fatigue in your legs, *reduce* the gear you are riding. If you find yourself breathing too hard, *increase* the gear. Proper attention to your gear ratio will result in the optimum relationship between energy expended and the speed maintained.

Riding Position

The three basic positions of the hands on the handlebars are reviewed in figures 22-1A to 22-4 on pages 232–36. Let's continue our analysis of positions to include the proper use of the body while riding the bicycle.

Maintaining a relaxed position is one of the key elements in cycling. Many people ride with their hands gripping the handlebars as if someone were trying to wrench the bars from their grip. Although you must maintain a grip on the bars, remember that the bicycle is designed to ride in a straight line without any effort except pedaling. If the bicycle requires your attention to ride in a straight line, something is probably misaligned. (Chapter 21 reviews the steps to insure that the frame is tracking correctly.) *You should not be expending energy on the bicycle unless it benefits your pedaling.* Imagine how tired you would be just sitting in your living room if you had a "death grip" on a pair of handlebars for two hours. *All* of your energy should be aimed at making the bicycle go faster; don't allow your energy to "run out" through your handlebars.

In all three handlebar positions (on the tops, behind the brake levers, and on the drops), the rider should have bent elbows. One

(continued on page 239)

Figures 22-1A, 22-1B: Handlebar Position 1. (A) The hands are placed on the "tops" of the handlebars. Always keep one hand in this position when riding one-handed—this position provides the greatest stability. (B) Variation on above position with hands a little further apart.

Figure 22-2: Handlebar Position 2. The hands are placed on the "tops" of the bars, behind the brake levers. This photograph demonstrates a variation of the position that is comfortable but does not permit the rider to reach the brake levers.

Figure 22-3: Handlebar Position 2A. Again, the hands are on the "tops," behind the brakes. However, this variation utilizes the top of the brake lever as a rest. All good-quality hand brakes include a rubber hood to insulate the hands against road shock. This position allows use of the brake by merely extending the fingers. This position is recommended for climbing when out of the saddle. This position is very stable, allows free breathing, and the levers can be used to increase pedal pressure when hill climbing.

Figure 22-4: Handlebar Position 3. Proper placement of the hands in this position varies according to the physique of the rider. There is one rule of thumb: The wrist should be straight. If you hold your wrist straight before you touch the bars and then grasp the bar at the spot where your wrist is straight, you have found the "correct" position.

Figure 22-5: *Incorrect* Position 3. The wrist is not straight and the hand is too close to the end of the handlebar. This position drastically reduces your control of the bicycle. Check for yourself. Try weaving back and forth with your hands in this position. Now try the same test with your hands correctly placed. The increase in stability should be immediately obvious.

237

Figure 22-6: *Incorrect* Position 3. Again the wrists are not straight; however, this time they are flexed the opposite direction as in figure 22-5. Although this position is fairly stable, it does not allow efficient use of the arm and shoulder muscles.

of the prime reasons that some riders find this uncomfortable is because the bicycle setup is incorrect. If you are experiencing difficulty in riding with your elbows bent (or you have specific neck or back pains when riding), review the portion of chapter 20 that details proper setup.

> *Rule of thumb:* If you want to go faster or apply more force to the pedals, increase the amount of bend in your elbows.

As outlined in chapter 20, the reason is simple—the powerful gluteus maximus comes into use as the back is bent below 45 degrees. There are two additional reasons why the elbows should be bent:

1. Bent elbows act as shock absorbers for your body. This shock absorber effect results in less abuse to the rider and to the bicycle. It reduces "pounding" on the elbow and shoulder joints and also relieves much of the strain that wheels are subjected to when crossing railroad tracks or hitting bumps.

2. Bent elbows provide a "safety buffer" in situations where a rider is bumped from the side by another rider. If a rider is riding with "locked" elbows and is bumped, the forks will react violently and increase the possibility of a spill. If the elbows are relaxed, any sideward force will be absorbed by the elbow and arm, not the bicycle.

> *Rule of thumb:* The wrist should be straight when using the drops of the handlebars.

Since the use of the bottom of the handlebars results in such a drastic body position, the drops should only be used under conditions of maximum output. Therefore, the arms should be using the handlebars to increase leverage and pedal pressure. In this situation, the only practical position to be able to pull effectively is when the wrist is straight. A useful analogy is the position of the arm and hand when lifting a barbell. It is obviously very difficult to lift with the wrist bent.

Normally, the hand will be located in the curve of the handlebars when the wrist is straight. Riding with the hand located at the back part of the bottom of the bar usually indicates that the rider is resting his weight on the bars. If the rider is resting his weight on the bars because it is the most comfortable position for the back, the *same* position of the upper body can be maintained if the hands are moved to Position 2 and the amount of bend in the elbows is increased. Position 2 will also provide the shock absorber effect without any loss of efficiency.

Many riders unconsciously perform miniature "push-ups" as they ride. This is an indication that the rider is not using the arms properly and it actually tires the rider more than if the upper body is kept relatively still. Imagine, for instance, how many of these miniature push-ups are performed during a two-hour ride. Now imagine sitting at home with your hands on a table performing the same push-ups for two hours. None of that energy expended was used to make the bicycle go faster. The push-ups are usually performed unconsciously by the rider, but they should be eliminated because they result in an energy loss without any increase in efficiency.

Pedaling

Strictly speaking, intentional "ankling" is incorrect in spite of the many books and magazine articles that tell of its benefits. None of the dozens of coaches that we have spoken to about pedaling advocate ankling. A review of the many good European cycling books will reveal that there is no mention of ankling as a benefit to cycling. The motion that has often been incorrectly described as ankling, is an exaggeration (or misunderstanding) of the motions used in walking. Let's review the motion of a person's foot during a single step before we discuss proper pedaling technique.

1. As the foot is lifted, the heel naturally precedes the toe in the upward motion of the leg. No one makes a conscious effort to raise the heel first. It moves first because the muscles controlling the foot are relaxed and the lifting motion of the leg is done by the muscles in the upper leg.

2. As the foot descends, the heel begins to lead the toe, in readiness to make contact with the ground, since the *heel will touch the ground first—not* the toe.

3. The heel touches the ground first and as the body moves forward the weight is transferred to the ball of the foot and the process continues. If one is to believe the proponents of ankling, the rider should move the toes of the foot down at the bottom of the pedal stroke. This is no more correct than it is to recommend the same motion when walking. Our muscles have functioned in a relatively fixed manner since we initially learned to walk—the most efficient pedal stroke utilizes the *natural motion* of the foot. The proponents of ankling are usually not cycling coaches. Instead, they are persons who have attempted to analyze the motions of the foot in the pedal stroke of the expert cyclist. It is easy to become misled when looking at the motions of a foot during the pedal stroke because, when a high rpm is maintained, the toe *will* precede the heel at the bottom of the stroke. It does not precede the heel because the rider consciously "pushes" the toe through first; it occurs because the centrifugal force of the high rpm's does not allow the full drop of the heel. The opposite is true in the use of a high gear at low rpm's—the heel will often be as low as the toes.

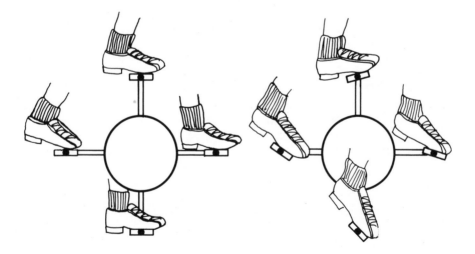

Figure 22-7: On the left, a more normal position of the foot through pedal arc. On the right, an exaggerated idea of the foot position on the pedal, which is held by many cyclists.

There is one foolproof method to determine if a rider is ankling or if his lower leg is operating properly—that is to watch the calf muscles expand and contract during the pedal stroke. Watching from behind, check to see when the calf is under pressure (tight). It should occur only on the down portion of the stroke. If the calf is tight on the up part of the stroke, the rider is still pushing with his toes instead of concentrating on *pulling* his whole foot up. Muscles "rest" by receiving fresh supplies of oxygenated blood; therefore, the rest period is greatest during the relaxed position of the muscle. Obviously, a muscle that is under tension during twice as much of the stroke will tire faster than a muscle that is given more opportunity to rest.

Although all serious cyclists have toe clips and straps on their pedals, most riders do not use them to their full advantage. You can prove this to yourself by watching the pedaling stroke of the average cyclist. Imagine the circle scribed by the cyclist's foot is the face of a clock. Most riders do not actually apply pressure to the pedals for more than three "hours" (from four to seven o'clock when the rider is viewed riding from left to right). It is impossible to assist individual riders with their pedal stroke in a book—that is the job of the coach. Understanding and being able to analyze the theory of efficient pedaling will hopefully benefit all riders who do not have a coach available.

Cornering

Although many riders have no intention of racing, learning how to corner at speed is important to reduce accidents. The tourist often requires these skills when descending mountains. There are two basic techniques for high-speed cornering— pedaling through the corner and coasting through the corner. Before a rider attempts to negotiate coasting through a corner at high speed, the method of efficiently pedaling through the corner should be mastered.

Pedaling through a corner

This method is important to master because it is necessary to achieve the proper position and confidence before attempting to learn the fastest way around a corner which is coasting. When pedaling around a righthand corner, the rider should attempt to keep the bicycle as upright as possible to reduce the possibility of hitting the pedal on the ground. To best accomplish this, the rider should bend the elbows slightly more than usual and move the upper body to the right until the rider's nose is approximately over the right hand. On lefthand corners, the procedure is reversed. The body should lean to the left with the rider's nose over the left hand.

Figure 22-8: Coasting through a corner at high speed requires a low center of gravity. Notice how both riders have shifted their weight to the *outside* crank which is positioned at the bottom of the stroke. The upper body of the rider is then moved slightly to the inside by aligning the rider's nose over the *inside* hand.

Coasting through a corner

To better understand why the recommended position is so effective, let's look at the two primary factors that act on the bicycle when cornering at speed—the center of gravity of the bicycle and the traction of the tires. The weight of the rider is primarily resting at the level of the bicycle seat. The amount of weight on the seat decreases, of course, as the rider increases pressure on the pedals. The traction of the tires is affected by the tire construction, road surface, weight of the bicycle and rider, and the centrifugal force caused by going through the turn. To increase cornering speed, the center of gravity of the bicycle must be lowered. That is best accomplished by placing the majority of the rider's weight on the pedals.

Specifically, a *right-hand* turn should be accomplished as follows:

- Rider's nose over right hand. (This means that if a plumb line were to be dropped from your nose, it should fall just over the right hand.)
- Inside crank (right foot is in uppermost position) should be in the *up* position.
- Outside crank (left foot is in lowest position) will be in the *down* position.
- Rider should concentrate his weight on the *outside* leg— effectively lowering the center of gravity as much as possible.

A *left-hand* corner is negotiated similarly:

- Rider's nose over *left* hand.
- Inside crank should be *up*.
- Outside crank should be *down*.
- Weight on *outside* leg.

Some riders prefer to allow the *inside* knee to drop from its normal position near the top tube for improved balance, however it is not required.

Crossing railroad tracks or large bumps

The rider should absorb the majority of shock transmitted by large bumps. To do this without rider discomfort, the hands should firmly grip the handlebars, the elbows should be well flexed, and the rider's weight should be concentrated on the pedals which are held stationary in a position parallel to the ground. This position reduces the deadweight that causes bent rims. It also lowers the center of gravity of the bicycle, and, similar to the technique used in motorcycle scrambles, the bicycle moves around freely under the rider with a minimum loss of control.

Riding with One Hand

Frequently the rider is required to remove one hand from the handlebars, whether it is to reach for a water bottle or signal for a turn. This can result in a potentially dangerous lack of control of the bicycle if not handled properly. The preferred method of one-handed riding can best be demonstrated by the riders in a six-day bicycle race. When the rider pushes his teammate into the race, he always has his hand on the top of the handlebar adjacent to the stem. With the hand near the center of the handlebars, the weight of the rider is as equally distributed on the handlebars as possible. To prove the benefits of this position, perform the following test: Ride one handed with your hand in Position 3 (at the bottom of the handlebars). Attempt a few swerves to the left and the right. Next, perform the same test with one hand in Position 2 on the handlebars. Finally, perform the swerve test with one hand in Position 1 on the handlebars. The difference in control between the three positions should be immediately obvious.

European Frame Builders

Additional information about products offered by the frame builders in this book can be obtained by writing directly to the builder. However, to expedite your inquiries the following U.S. importers can be of assistance.

Condor

Georgetown Cycle Sport
Wildwood Manor Shopping Center
Bethesda, MD 20014
301-530-9011

Paris Sport Cycle
186 Main Street
Ridgefield Park, NJ 07660
201-641-0087

Bob Jackson, Mercian

Bikecology Bike Shops
3910 Nebraska Avenue
PO Box 1880
Santa Monica, CA 90406
213-829-7681

Jack Taylor

Fulton Street Cyclery
3038 Fulton Street
San Francisco, CA 94118
415-387-4978

Bud's Bike Shop
217 West First Street
Claremont, CA 91711
714-626-3285

Roberts Cycle Company
7053 North Clark Street
Chicago, IL 60626
312-274-9281

Raleigh

Raleigh Industries of
America, Inc.
1170 Commonwealth Avenue
Boston, MA 02134
617-734-0240

Guerciotti, Pogliaghi, Woodrup
Ten Speed Drive Imports, Inc.
PO Box 2152
1403 South Patrick Drive
Indian Harbour Beach, FL 32937
305-773-8654

Gitane

Gitane Pacific
4925 West 147th Street
Hawthorne, CA 90250
213-644-8651

Peugeot

Cycles Peugeot U.S.A.,
Inc.
540 East Alondra
Boulevard
Gardena, CA 90247
213-774-5454
or
213-537-3600

Cinelli

Ultima
PO Box 37426
Houston, TX 77036
713-661-9132

American Frame Builders

The following is a list of some of the experienced American frame builders who have acquired, or are developing, good reputations through the quality of their frame building. We apologize for any omissions; we assembled the list from our personal experience or recommendations from persons whose opinions we respect.

Francisco Cuevas
c/o Paris Sport Cycle
186 Main Street
Ridgefield Park, NJ 07660

Bruce Gordon Cycles
27729 Clear Lake Road
Eugene, OR 97402

Custom Cycles by Wm.
    Sampson
5052 Corbin Avenue
San Jose, CA 95118

Jim Redcay
PO Box 62
Washington Street
Lambertville, NJ 08530

Colin Laing Racing Cycles
917 East Fort Lowell
Tucson, AZ 85719

TREK Bicycle Corporation
268 Jackson Street
Waterloo, WI 53594

Bill Boston Cycles
38 Franklin Street
PO Box 114
Swedesboro, NJ 08085

Strawberry Racing Cycles,
    Inc.
510 NW Third Avenue
Portland, OR 97209

F. M. Assenmacher Light-
    weight Cycles
104 East May Street
Mount Pleasant, MI 48858

Proteus Design
9225 Baltimore Boulevard
College Park, MD 20740

Caylor Frames
519 Kansas Avenue
Modesto, CA 95350

Recommended Brazing Procedures*

1. Before the tubes are assembled the ends should be degreased and cleaned with emery over the area which is inserted into the lug. This ensures that the brazing material makes good contact with the parent metal. (Reynolds 531 cycle tubes are sent out free from scale and rust, and protected with an anticorrosive oil, but if by some mischance during transport or storage some rust should form, this must be completely removed.)

2. When the tubes are fitted into the lugs and pegged, care should be taken that the assembly is not in a state of stress.

3. Brazing should be carried out in the following clockwise sequence:

   a. Bottom bracket
   b. Down tube and head tube joint
   c. Head tube and top tube joint
   d. Top tube and seat tube joint.

   This sequence obviates the danger of a stress raiser being created at a major shock point.

4. When brazing frames made from Reynolds 531 tubing, the joints should be preheated, and after brazing the cooling should be controlled. Brazing must be carried out in a shop free from drafts.

5. We prefer the torch brazing method as this reduces the risk of overheating the material and causes less distortion, thus reducing subsequent setting times. The hearth method of brazing can also be used, but whatever method is used, great care must be taken not to overheat the material, or to heat too large an

---

(Courtesy of TI Reynolds)

area of the tube. Overheating will lead to burning or to brass inclusion (where the molten brass or bronze enters the grain of the steel), either of which will make the tube brittle.

6. Setting, when necessary, should always be done cold.

7. Most proprietary brazing materials can be used satisfactorily, but we recommend the use of brazing materials with a melting point of about 850°C. (1,562°F.).

APPENDIX IV

Bottom Bracket Width

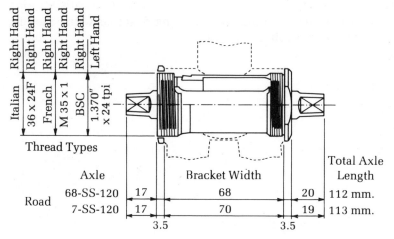

Axle	Bracket Width	Total Axle Length
Road	68-SS-120	17	68	20	112 mm.
	7-SS-120	17	70	19	113 mm.

3.5   3.5

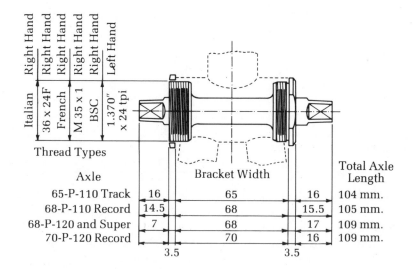

Axle	Bracket Width	Total Axle Length
65-P-110 Track	16	65	16	104 mm.
68-P-110 Record	14.5	68	15.5	105 mm.
68-P-120 and Super	7	68	17	109 mm.
70-P-120 Record		70	16	109 mm.

3.5   3.5

252

Chain Lines

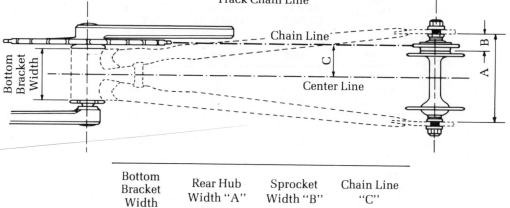

Bottom Bracket Width	Rear Hub Width "A"	Sprocket Width "B"	Chain Line "C"
65	110	21.5	40
68	110	21.5	40
68	120	24	42.5
70	120	24	42.5

Road Chain Line

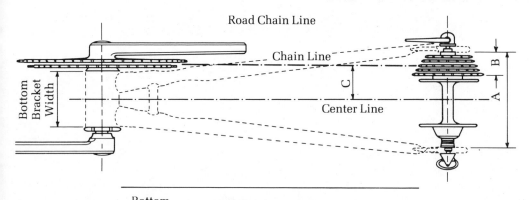

Bottom Bracket Width	Rear Hub Width "A"	Freewheel Width "B"	Chain Line "C"
68	120	29	43.5
70	120	29	43.5
74	120	29	43.5

Tandem Chain Line

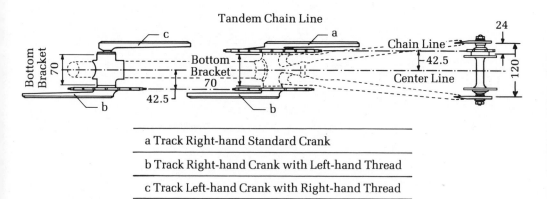

a Track Right-hand Standard Crank

b Track Right-hand Crank with Left-hand Thread

c Track Left-hand Crank with Right-hand Thread

Glossary

Agrati—an Italian company that produces many frame-building parts such as bottom brackets, lugs, and dropouts.

anodized—metal subjected to electrolytic action to coat it with a protective and/or decorative finish.

baking oven—a large structure with variable temperature controls that is used to bake paint finishes on bicycle frames.

balloon tire—a tire 2 or more inches wide with a low pressure capacity.

bearing race—the circle that the balls in bearing cones and cups make as they contact the axle.

Bivalent hub—a Cinelli-designed hub for bicycle wheels. Bivalent hubs permit a quick rear-wheel change since the freewheel remains with the frame—not with the hub. Front and rear wheels are interchangeable. Unfortunately, because of high production costs, Cino Cinelli has withdrawn the hubs from the market.

bottom bracket—a short round tube on a bicycle frame to which the down tube, seat tube, and chainstays have been brazed or welded.

bottom bracket cup—a part of the bottom bracket bearings that screws into the frame's bottom bracket and in which the crank axle's bearings run.

bottom tube (on tandem)—tube connecting the two cranksets.

brazing—a process by which two metal surfaces are joined by means of heating and melting a third substance such as brass or silver.

brazing with pins—the use of "nails" in frame construction to keep the tubes in the proper position in the lugs.

bronze brazing—melting bronze in order to join two metal surfaces that have higher melting temperatures than the bronze.

Brox—French brazing material used in frame building.

butted tubing—catchall term given to all tubes that are either double butted, single butted, or taper gauge.

    a. double butted—refers to a tube that is thicker at the ends than in the middle without an increase in its outside diameter.

    b. single butted—same as double butted, except only one end is thicker.

    c. taper gauge—refers to a tube whose thickness is gradually diminished through highly mechanized industrial operations. Forks are always either taper gauge or straight gauge; they are never double butted or single butted.

Campi—term used when referring to components made by S.P.A. Brevetti Internazionali Campagnolo.

carbon fiber—a chemical term which refers to a composite of fibers of a pure element, in this case carbon, that are woven and distributed randomly and are bound together to form a strong lightweight material.

cast bottom bracket—a bottom bracket that is formed in a mold and, as a result, does not have a seam.

caster—a word used interchangeably with tail and trail. Caster angle is formed by the intersection of a vertical line drawn through the front fork ends and a line which is parallel to the head tube and is extended to the wheelbase.

cast lug—a bicycle lug that is formed in a mold and, consequently, does not have seams.

Castolin—a brazing material with about 40 percent silver produced by the Swiss firm, La Castolin Société Anonyme of Lausanne.

cast seat lug—seatpost lug molded to precision.

century—100-mile ride.

chainstays—two tubes which go from the bottom bracket to the rear dropouts.

chrome plating—applying a thin coating of chromium on frames or other bicycle parts.

cold setting—aligning frame while it is cold (after brazing).

Columbus—Italian-produced special frame tubing.

cone and locknut—bearing parts that attach to axle on which bearings run around. The nut is screwed down hard on another nut to prevent slacking back.

Continental fork section—refers to wide oval fork blades.

copper-tacked or coppered—initial step in frame-building procedures in which tubes and lugs are held together by torching copper.

crankarm—rotating portion which holds the pedal.

criterium—a multilap road race that is held on a short circuit varying in length from one to ten miles. The criterium course utilizes public roads that are temporarily closed to normal traffic. This race is designed to allow the spectator to see the riders as they pass by each lap.

custom frame—bicycle frame that is built by an artisan to fit the various needs of the individual customer.

cyclo-cross—cross-country race event on special course featuring obstacles.

derailleur—a mechanical device that is bolted to the bicycle frame. Its purpose is to shift (or derail) the chain from one gear to another, allowing variable gear ratios.

down tube—that part of the bicycle frame which connects the bottom of the head tube with the bottom bracket.

drop-forged handlebar stem—stem made from aluminum alloy and forged to shape under high pressure.

dropouts—slots into which the front and rear wheels fit.

ergonomics—biotechnology or the application of biological and engineering data to problems related to man and machine.

faced bottom bracket—edges of the bottom bracket are faced with a special tool to make sure that they are squared.

facing—squaring edges with a special tool.

flash-weld—using heavy electrical current at high speed and frequency to weld tubes.

flat top crown—a fork crown on which the top part is flat.

fork—that part of the bicycle that holds the front wheel in place and is attached to the frame by the headset. The fork assembly includes a fork steering column, a fork crown, fork blades, and the fork dropouts. There are three types: semi-sloping, fully sloping, and flat.

fork blades—curved tubes that connect the fork crown to the front dropouts which hold the front wheel in place.

fork crown—that part of the fork that attaches the fork blades to the fork steering column.
   a. stamped or pressed—fork crown which has been cut, bent, and stamped into shape by a die.
   b. forged—a fork crown that is produced with the grain of the steel "in line" by heating and hammering with highly refined machines.
   c. cast—similar to the cast lugs and the cast bottom bracket, the cast fork crown is formed in a mold and, as a result, does not have a seam.

fork rake—each bicycle fork is bent or curved on the bottom, just before it attaches to the fork dropouts. The fork rake is the amount the tube is bent.

freewheel—a mechanism with one, two, three, four, five, six, or even seven individual sprockets with varying numbers of teeth on each sprocket. The freewheel threads onto the rear hub and, together with the chain and crankset, permits the rider to propel his bicycle. The various number of teeth on the freewheel sprockets determines the gear ratios for a particular bicycle. The name "freewheel" is given to this gear mechanism because it is built to enable the rider to coast when not pedaling, as opposed to a direct-driven mechanism which requires the cyclist to pedal all the time.

front-wheel expander brake—brake with a hub shell and an internal expanding brake shoe.

gear ratio—To calculate a gear ratio, multiply the diameter of the wheel in inches by the number of teeth on the front chainwheel and then divide by the number of teeth on the rear sprocket. For a 10-speed these calculations must be done ten different times; once for each of the different chainwheel/freewheel sprocket combinations. Gear ratios can also be calculated in meters.

glass beading—cleaning the surface of a metal with tiny glass beads propelled by a jet of compressed air.

Haden blank—an oversize lug manufactured by Haden Brothers, Limited, of Birmingham, England. It is intended for the builder who wishes to file the lug to a final shape that varies from those commercially available.

hanger bracket—another name for bottom bracket.

head angle—refers to the angle which is formed by drawing a straight line through the head tube to the ground.

headset—parts of bearing mechanism in the head tube that secure the fork to the main triangle.

high-wheeler—bicycles of the late 1800s with large-diameter front wheels (approximately 50 inches) and smaller-diameter rear wheels (approximately 17 inches), straight handlebars, and spokes radiating directly from the hub (no crossover); vehicle was mounted via a small step above the rear wheel.

hot setting—aligning frame while it is still hot.

investment cast lug—mold is made of lug to precision then filled with wax. The wax is melted out, leaving the mold to be filled with the material for the lug.

Italian section fork—a term synonymous with the large, sectioned fork blades.

jig—a metal fixture that firmly holds various frame parts while the builder brazes them together.

lug—metal sleeve that holds the frame tubes at the joints.

lug cutout—designed pattern that is incorporated into the lug.

main triangle—that part of the frame which is made up of the head tube, top tube, seat tube, and the down tube.

mandrel—a spindle or metal bar around which tubes are shaped.

mass start race—any race on either the track or road where the competitors start at the same time.

microfusione—term used in describing investment cast products.

mitered tube—a tube which has been precisely cut so that the entire diameter of the tube sits flush against the tube it butts up against.

Nervex—the brand name of quality lugs, bottom brackets, and fork crowns produced by the French company Ets. Aimé Dubois in Yssingeaux, France.

pannier—saddlebag that is mounted on a bicycle by means of a carrier over the rear or front wheel. It is generally constructed of heavy-duty canvas or reinforced nylon.

pinning—drilling holes through tubes and lugs and inserting wire pins or "nails" to hold alignment during brazing.

pinstriping—decorative paint trimming on tubes.

plain gauge tubing—tubes in which the walls are of uniform thickness.

pressed steel lug—a lug which has been cut, bent, and stamped into shape by a die.

Prugnat—the brand name of quality lugs, bottom brackets, and fork crowns produced by the French company of the same name located in Moret-sur-Loing, France.

pursuit—track race with two competitors (individuals or teams) starting simultaneously on opposite sides of the track and trying to catch one another.

quick-release mechanism—a device used to quickly tighten or loosen a cable, wheel, or seat without the use of any wrenches.

racing frame—a frame designed for performance rather than comfort.

Reynolds tubing—the name of the tubing produced by TI Reynolds, the world's largest manufacturer of quality bicycle tubing.
  a. 531DB—tubing made of manganese-molybdenum steel. This designation usually refers to the fact that the entire frame is built with the appropriate butted tubings.
  b. 531SL—same as the 531DB except that the gauges are lighter, making the tubing "Special Lightweight."
  c. 753—also a manganese-molybdenum steel butted tubing. The tubing wall has been reduced in thickness to make it lighter than the 531SL, yet its composition makes it 50 percent stronger. A frame built with 753 is generally 20 percent lighter than one built with 531SL.

ring-braze—inserting a ring of brass between the tube and the lug when brazing.

Roto—an Italian firm that produces frame-building parts such as fork crowns, lugs, and bottom brackets; especially known for their investment cast products.

saddle angle—the tilt of the saddle as it is positioned on the seatpost.

saddle height—the distance from the top of the saddle to the top of the pedal when it is near the bottom of its rotation as it is in line with the seat tube.

safety bicycle—bicycle with wheels of equal size and with a chain gearing setup so that the wheels go faster than the pedals.

seatstays—two tubes that run from the top of the seat tube to the rear dropouts.

    a. fully wrap—seatstays that are attached and wrapped around the front of the seat lug as far as possible. The two ends of the seatstays are then connected by filling the space with braze.

    b. semi-wrap—seatstays are attached to the side of the seat lug.

    c. fastback—seatstays that butt up against the seat tube or are attached to the rear of the seat lug.

seat tube—the tube running from the top tube to the down tube.

seat tube angle—the angle formed by the seat tube and the ground.

sew-up tire—a tire in which the inner tube has been stitched inside the tire's casing. This tire is always glued onto the rim.

side-loading—force perpendicular to center line of frame caused by off-center foot pressure on the pedals.

Sifbronze—name used when referring to brazing materials made by Sifbronze, a division of Suffolk Lawn Mowers, Limited, in Suffolk, England.

silver solder—any braze material with a high mixture of silver.

spoke nipple—tip that is inserted through the rim and is threaded onto the spoke.

spot tack—joining the lugs and tubes together by brazing in various spots before a final brazing of the joint. This method is used as a preliminary step in the brazing process since it allows for easy corrections if any misalignment is noted.

standard drawn tubing—tubing accurately sized by drawing over a mandrel.

stove-enamel finish—another name for a baked-on enamel finish.

stress—a force being applied on a frame and the frame's ability to resist it.

Super Vitus—quality butted tubing produced by Ateliers de la Rive in Sainte Chamond, France.

tack brazing—same as spot tacking.

tensile strength—the greatest stress a substance can bear without disintegrating or breaking.

threads—the size and number of threads per inch that appear on a fork column and in the bottom bracket.
  a. English—an English fork column has a headset with a 1-inch opening and 24 threads per inch (1″ x 24 tpi). An English bottom bracket has cups that are 1.370 inches wide with 24 threads per inch (1.370″ x 24 tpi). The adjustable cup has right-handed threads while the fixed cup has left-handed threads. English-threaded components are sometimes referred to as having BSC threads.
  b. French—a French fork column requires a headset with a 25-mm. opening with 1 thread per millimeter or 25.4 threads per inch (25 mm. x 1.0 mm.). A French bottom bracket has cups that are 35 mm. wide with 25.4 threads per inch (35 mm. x 1.0 mm.). Both the adjustable and the fixed cups have right-handed threads.
  c. Italian—an Italian-threaded fork column would require a headset with a 25.4-mm. opening with 24 threads per inch (25.4 mm. x 24 tpi). An Italian bottom bracket has cups that are 36 mm. wide with 24 threads per inch (36 mm. x 24 tpi). Both the adjustable and the fixed cups have right-handed threads.
  d. Swiss—same as French threads except the fixed cup on the bottom bracket has left-handed threads.

titanium—a grey, lightweight metal used in frame construction and in the manufacture of high-quality components.

toe clip—metal piece attached to front of pedal which secures the foot, and together with a strap, buckles around the middle of the foot for increased pedaling efficiency.

top eye—small fitting that is inserted and brazed on semi-wrapped seatstays.

top tube—the tube on a frame that connects the head tube to the seat tube.

touring frame—frame designed for comfort and stability when laden with touring packs.

tracking—making sure that wheels are both in a direct line and parallel from front to rear.

tubing gauge—the thickness of tubes.

tubular tire—another name for a sew-up tire.

wheelbase—the distance from the center of the bicycle's front wheel to the center of its rear wheel.

Bibliography

Ald, Roy. *Cycling: The Rhythmic, Respiratory Way to Physical Fitness.* New York: Grosset & Dunlap, 1968.

Alth, Max. *All about Bikes and Bicycling: Care, Repair, and Safety.* New York: Hawthorn Books, 1972.

Arkhipov, Evenii, and Sedov, A. *Na Olimpiĭskih Trekah* [On Olympic Tracks]. Moscow: Sovietskaya Rossiya, 1961.

————. *Odnodnevnye Shosseĭnye Gonki* [Short, One Day Road Pursuits]. Moscow: Fizikultura i Sport, 1960.

————. *Velosipenye Gonki po Shosse* [Bicycle Pursuit on the Road]. Moscow: Fizikultura i Sport, 1958.

Asa, Warren. *American Youth Hostels' North American Bicycle Atlas.* 3rd ed. New York: American Youth Hostels, 1973.

Ballantine, Richard. *Richard's Bicycle Book.* New York: Ballantine Books, 1974.

Baranet, Nancy Neiman. *Bicycling: The Bicycle in Recreation, Competition, Transportation.* South Brunswick, N.J.: A. S. Barnes, 1973.

————. *The Turned Down Bar.* Philadelphia: Dorrance, 1964.

Bastide, Roger. *A la Pointe des Pelotons* [At the Head of the Pack]. Paris: Solar, 1972.

————. *A la Pointe des Pelotons: Ocana Face à Merckx* [At the Head of the Pack: Ocana Facing Merckx]. Paris: Presses Pocket, 1974.

————. *Doping*. Paris: Solar, 1970.

Belt, Forest H., and Mahoney, Richard. *Bicycle Maintenance & Repair: Brakes, Chains, Derailleurs*. Indianapolis, Ind.: T. Audel, 1975.

————. *Bicycle Maintenance & Repair: Frames, Tires, Wheels*. Indianapolis, Ind.: T. Audel, 1975.

Bike World. Bicycle Track Racing. Mountain View, Calif.: Bike World Publications, 1977.

Bobet, Jean. *La Course en Tête* [The Race Up Front]. Paris: La Table Ronde, 1966.

Boethling, Bob, ed. *The Bicycle Book*. Los Angeles: Price, Stern, & Sloan, 1972.

Bowden, Gregory Houston. *The Story of the Raleigh Cycle*. London: W. H. Allen, 1975.

Bowden, Kenneth. *Cycle Racing*. London: Temple Press, 1958.

Bridge, Raymond. *Freewheeling: The Bicycle Camping Book*. Harrisburg, Pa.: Stackpole Books, 1974.

Browder, Sue. *The American Biking Atlas & Touring Guide*. New York: Workman Publishing, 1974.

Burstyn, Ben. *Bicycle Repair & Maintenance*. New York: Arco, 1974.

Central Sports School (C.O.N.I.). *Cycling*. Rome: F.I.A.C., 1972.

Cuthbertson, Tom. *Anybody's Bike Book: An Original Manual of Bicycle Repairs*. Berkeley, Calif.: Ten Speed Press, 1971.

DeLong, Fred. *DeLong's Guide to Bicycles & Bicycling: The Art & Science*. rev. ed. Radnor, Pa., Chilton Book Co., 1978.

Dirand, Georges. *Poulidor*. Paris: Calmann-Levy, 1974.

Engel, Lyle K. *Bicycling for Fun & Health*. New York: Arco, 1975.

Hawkins, Karen and Gary. *Bicycle Touring in France*. London: Sidgwick & Jackson, 1974.

Henderson, N. G. *Continental Cycle Racing*. London: Pelham, 1970.

———. *Cyclepedia*. Silsden, England: Kennedy Brothers, 1971.

———. *Cycling Classics, 1970–72*. London: Pelham, 1973.

———. *Rainbow Jersey*. Silsden, England: Kennedy Brothers, 1970.

Humphrey, Clifford C. *Back to the Bike: How to Buy, Maintain, & Use the Bicycle as an Alternative Means of Transportation*. San Francisco: 101 Publications, 1972.

Jeuniau, Marc. *Le Cyclisme, de Coppi a VanLooy et Anquetil* [Cycling from Coppi to VanLooy and Anquetil]. Paris: Dargaud, 1967.

Kingbay, Keith. *Inside Bicycling*. Chicago: Regnery, 1977.

Kleeberg, Irene. *Bicycle Touring*. New York: Watts, 1975.

Kossack, Joe. *A Close-up Look at Bicycle Frames*. Mountain View, Calif.: World Publications, 1975.

Leete, Harley M., ed. *The Best of Bicycling!* New York: Trident Press, 1970.

Luebbers, David J. *The 1975 Bicycle Bibliography: Professional Supplement*. Denver, Colo.: by the author, 1976.

McCullagh, James C., ed. *American Bicycle Racing*. Emmaus, Pa.: Rodale Press, 1976.

Messenger, Charles. *Conquer the World*. London: Pelham, 1968.

———. *Where There's a Wheel*. London: Pelham, 1972.

Mohn, Peter. *Bicycle Touring.* Mankato, Minn.: Crestwood House, 1975.

Porter, Hugh. *Champion on Two Wheels.* London: R. Hale, 1975.

Proteus, Paul. *The Proteus Framebuilding Handbook.* College Park, Md.: Proteus Press, 1975.

Rebour, Daniel. *Cycles de Compétition et Randonneuses* [Racing and Touring Cycles]. Paris: Technique & Vulgarisation, 1976.

Ritchie, Andrew. *King of the Road.* London: Wildwood House, 1975.

Roth, Mark, and Walters, Sally. *Bicycling Through England.* New York: H. Z. Walck, 1976.

St. Pierre, Roger. *The Book of the Bicycle.* London: Ward Lock, 1973.

Saunders, David. *Cycling in the Sixties.* London: Pelham, 1971.

Schad, Jerry, and Krupp, Don. *Fifty Southern California Bicycle Trips.* Beaverton, Ore.: Touchstone Press, 1976.

Schwinn, Arnold & Company. *50 Years of Schwinn-Built Bicycles.* Chicago: by the author, 1945.

Shaw, Reginald C., ed. *The Raleigh Book of Cycling.* London: P. Davis, 1975.

Simes, Jack, and George, Barbara. *Winning Bicycle Racing.* Chicago: Regnery, 1976.

Simpson, Tommy. *Cycling Is My Life.* London: S. Paul, 1966.

Sloane, Eugene D. *The Complete Book of Cycling.* New York: Trident Press, 1970.

Sutherland, Howard. *Sutherland's Handbook for Bicycle Mechanics.* Berkeley, Calif.: Sutherland Publications, 1974.

U.S. Army Missile Command. *Human Engineering Design Data Digest.* Redstone, Ala.: Research and Engineering Directorate, 1969.

Urquhart, David I. *The Bicycle & How It Works.* New York: H. Z. Walck, 1972.

Wadley, J. B. *Cycling.* London: Macmillan, 1975.

Ward, Peter. *King of Sports: Cycle Road Racing.* Yorkshire, England: Kennedy Brothers, 1968.

Whiter, Robert. *The Bicycle Manual on Maintenance & Repairs.* Hollywood, Calif.: Laurida Books Pub. Co., 1972.

Wolfe, Frederick L. *Bicycle Denver: 107 Bicycle Tours.* Denver: Graphic Impressions, 1976.

Woodland, Les. *Cycle Racing: Training to Win.* London: Pelham, 1975.

Index

268